T0341378

THE UNIVERSITY OF MICHIGAN
CENTER FOR CHINESE STUDIES

MICHIGAN PAPERS IN CHINESE STUDIES
NO. 43

THE ECONOMIC DEVELOPMENT OF MANCHURIA: THE RISE OF A FRONTIER ECONOMY

by

Kang Chao

Ann Arbor

Center for Chinese Studies
The University of Michigan

1982

Library of Congress Cataloging in Publication Data

Chao, Kang, 1929–
    The economic development of Manchuria.
    (Michigan papers in Chinese studies; no. 43)
    Bibliography: p.
    1. Manchuria—Economic conditions. I. Title.
II. Series.
HC428.M3C355   1983   338.951'8   83-7455
ISBN 0-89264-043-X

Printed in the United States of America

CONTENTS

PREFACE

"The Economic Development of Manchuria: The Rise of a Frontier Economy" was written as an "interim research report, a summary and preliminary analysis of findings based on a larger study still under way." Although the study could not be completed, most of the work on the period between 1924 and 1941 had been completed at the time of publication of the article. We are now publishing the materials that include the detailed sectoral estimates that are referred to in the article (sections A-0). Some of the tables from the article have been revised in these sections, and the figures presented in sections A-O are the final estimates. "The Economic Development of Manchuria" article, reprinted by permission of the *Journal of Economic History*, has been reprinted in full except for minor modifications in style.

THE ECONOMIC DEVELOPMENT OF MANCHURIA:
The Rise of a Frontier Economy*

Introduction

The paper we are presenting here is in essence an interim research report, a summary and preliminary analysis of findings based on a larger study still under way. Thus, both the findings and the interpretations are subject to revision as we continue and complete our investigation.

The economic development of Manchuria holds special fascination, since within the compass of a limited area and a self-contained time span of about one hundred years—between 1860 and 1960—we witness three different types of development patterns, based on three alternative sources of economic growth. The first and longest period, extending roughly from 1860 to 1930, was based on the development of an open frontier, the settlement of a new region. Application of the staple theory of growth to Manchurian conditions can help to illuminate the character of the growth process during this first period. In this connection the Manchurian development case invites comparison with growth processes in other newly settled regions, for example, the U.S., Canada, and Australia.

Industrialization based to a considerable extent on the importation of foreign capital and entrepreneurship—primarily from Japan—provided the principal engine of growth during the second period, which extended roughly to the end of World War II. Growth during this period lends itself to some very interesting comparisons with other cases of colonial development within both the Japanese Empire (that is, Formosa and Korea) and territories governed by other powers. Accelerated industrialization (but based on greatly stepped-up domestic input mobilization, supplemented by Soviet credits and technical assistance) characterized growth during the last period, starting around 1950.

* We wish to acknowledge the invaluable research assistance of K. S. Liao and Nick Lardy in compiling tables 1 and 2 and appendix tables I-III, respectively. We would also like to thank the National Science Foundation, Social Science Research Council, and the University of Michigan Center for Chinese Studies for their support, without which this study could not have been undertaken.

1

The rise in the pace of input mobilization was, in turn, brought about through profound institutional change and transformation of the whole economic system. Through this transformation, state organs gained far-reaching control over the process of resource allocation and used this control to significantly raise the rate of saving and investment.

A study of Manchurian development is of potential analytic interest from an entirely different but related vantage point as well. It presents a sharp contrast to the development pattern in China Proper, a contrast between rapid development of a newly settled region and quite slow growth in a typical underdeveloped agrarian economy subject to acute population pressure. Given this contrasting development pattern, Manchuria's importance in the Chinese economy as a whole rose consistently and appreciably. Thus, one of the questions to be explored is: What role did Manchuria play, and how major an asset did it constitute in the development of the Chinese economy after 1950, when this region was reunited with China Proper?

Limitations of time and space preclude dealing with all of these questions and aspects within the confines of this paper. Therefore we will concentrate on an analysis of developments during the first two periods. Moreover, since our studies of the first period are still in the early stages of exploration, our analysis will necessarily be tentative and preliminary. For the second period, we have completed studies of the growth patterns and will therefore present an analysis of our findings. However, we have not yet completed our study of the sources of economic growth so that this subject will have to be deferred for later consideration.

Expansion of Manchuria's Agricultural Frontier, 1860–1930

The year 1860 represents a logical starting date for the study of Manchuria's modern economic growth for a number of reasons. It marks another turning point in the policy barring Manchuria to agricultural settlement by Chinese. Equally important, the Sino-Russian Treaty of Peking was signed that year, and this was soon followed by the opening of Newchwang, the first treaty port in Manchuria.[1] The opening of this port clearly marks the beginning of a continuous and sustained rise in the volume of exports.

The Ch'ing dynasty's Manchurian settlement policy was based on some mutually conflicting considerations. The early Manchu emperors favored a policy aiming at the preservation of the frontier's political and cultural status quo. Chinese immigration was prohibited in the pursuit of this objective. The

---

[1] J. K. Fairbank, E. O. Reischauer, and A. Craig, *East Asia: The Modern Transformation* (Boston: Houghton Mifflin, 1965), p. 173.

Manchu rulers not only wanted to prevent the sinification of the frontier but also wished to safeguard the exclusive Manchu right to exploit three of the region's most highly valued products: ginseng, furs, and pearls. The emperors were also very much concerned about protecting the frontier from foreign incursion, that is, Russian expansion and pressure from "barbarians."[2]

With this in mind, they were most anxious to preserve the military prowess of the Manchu frontier bannermen. However, this whole policy proved unsuccessful, since the frontier Manchus, despite subsidies and other incentives, were continually tempted away to the life of ease and privilege in Peking. As a result, there was an ever-present threat of depopulation in Manchuria. To counter this threat and to fill the emerging power vacuum, Manchu emperors relaxed the prohibitions on Chinese immigration from time to time. Consequently, Chinese settled in these frontier regions—in part legally and in part illegally—throughout the period of Ch'ing rule even prior to 1860. That year, amid the Taiping Rebellion, the greatly weakened dynasty sanctioned once more the sale of land in Manchuria to Chinese as a means of raising revenues and producing land taxes.[3] The Hulan district in Heilungkiang Province and the Lalin district in Kirin Province were both opened to Chinese settlement in 1860. Gradually other districts were similarly opened in subsequent years, until all remaining restrictions were lifted for Kirin in 1902 and for Heilungkiang in 1904.[4]

Although 1860 represents a logical starting point for the study of Manchurian economic development, this task is greatly complicated by the paucity and unreliability of the data available for the nineteenth century. Both analytically and datawise, the 1860 to 1930 period can be subdivided into at least two phases: the periods before and after the completion of the Chinese Eastern Railway and the South Manchurian Railway between 1901 and 1903.[5] Another significant turning point is the founding of the South Manchurian Railway Company with Japanese capital in 1907. The S.M.R. Company operated this railway after it was ceded to the Japanese by the Russians following the end of the Russo-Japanese War in 1905. The S.M.R. evolved into

---

[2] This brief discussion of the sinicization of the Manchurian frontier is largely based on the study by Robert H. G. Lee, *The Manchurian Frontier in Ch'ing History* (Cambridge, Mass.: Harvard University Press, 1970). See especially pp. 20-23.

[3] K. C. Sun, *The Economic Development of Manchuria in the First Half of the Twentieth Century* (Cambridge, Mass.: Harvard University Press, 1969), p. 11.

[4] Robert Lee, *Frontier*, p. 103.

[5] See David J. Dallin, *The Rise of Russia in Asia* (New Haven: Yale University Press, 1949); and S. H. Chou, "Railway Development and Economic Growth in Manchuria," *The China Quarterly* 45 (January-March 1971): table III, p. 63.

a holding company with a number of subsidiary enterprises and with a sizable economic research department. The latter began compiling and publishing a basic economic series starting with 1907. Moreover, in 1907 three new ports were opened by treaty—Antung, Dairen, and Tatungkow—thus breaking the foreign trade monopoly of the port of Newchwang.[6] For all of these reasons the data prior to 1907 are distinctly inferior to those for the subsequent years and are not fully comparable either in quality or in coverage.

During this phase of Manchuria's economic growth, we witness the rapid settlement of "empty lands." Between 1860 and the early 1900s, the principal sources of growth were population expansion and extension of the land under cultivation, reinforced by marked growth in foreign trade. In the absence of output data for this period, it is uncertain whether or not this was a clear case of export-led growth, since we have no way of estimating whether exports rose more rapidly than domestic output. It is clear, as will be shown below, that export expansion outpaced the rate of increase in the principal inputs (land and labor), but whether the same can be said of outputs is unclear.

Soybeans, soybean cake, and soybean oil dominated exports, so much so that in 1872 these constituted close to 90 percent of total sales abroad. By 1899 and 1906 this diminished somewhat to about 80 percent. (See tables 3 and 4.) Prior to the advent of the railroad, these soybeans and soybean products were shipped to the port of Newchwang either on rivers or overland. The Liao was navigable for about 400 miles, but only by junks, since the presence of shoals prevented navigation by larger vessels. The same can be said of most of the other rivers, although the Amur and Sungari were navigable by steamboat over longer distances. All of these rivers were ice-bound for four to six months, but could serve as highways for overland traffic during the winter season.[7]

We see then a pattern of development emerging in the second half of the nineteenth century triggered on the one hand by the opening of Manchuria to land settlement by Chinese and on the other by the simultaneous opening of the first seaport to foreign trade. These twin developments served to mutually reinforce each other as immigration spurred land settlement, and the combination of the two led to rapid agricultural expansion.

The demand stimulus for this agricultural expansion was provided by two interacting sources. The consumption needs of a rapidly rising population had to be provided for, and this in turn was reflected in the rapid growth of farm staples—principally kaoliang and other grains. At the same time, the continuous rise in the export demand of soybeans and bean products encouraged

[6] Bank of Chosen, *The Economic History of Manchuria* (Seoul, 1920), pp. 204-5.
[7] Ibid., pp. 17, 213; see also Theodore Shabad, *China's Changing Map* (New York: Praeger, 1972), p. 246.

a sustained increase in soybean acreage and production. The proceeds from this crop provided a major source of cash income to the farm population which then stimulated a further rise in consumption demand for grain staples, for consumer goods imports, and for domestically supplied services. Increasing demands for agricultural products stimulated further immigration, land settlement, and population growth, which in turn led to a continuing rise in farm production and a mutually reinforcing pattern of economic growth. Some of these relationships can be documented, as will be shown below. Others can only be inferred due to lack of data.

It would seem that this growth process may have been accelerated after the completion of the two major railways in 1901 and 1903 and their official opening to traffic in 1903 and 1907, respectively. The Chinese Eastern, completed first, cut across Manchuria from west to east and linked the Transsiberian Railway with Vladivostok, a total length of 1,067 miles. The South Manchurian Railway then linked Harbin to the seaport of Dairen, a length of about 690 miles.[8] In the same year that the S.M.R. became fully operational, Dairen was opened to foreign trade and then or within the subsequent two years a number of inland cities—some located on rivers and others on the major railroad lines—became treaty ports in which internal and foreign trade could be carried on both by Chinese and foreign residents.[9]

The opening of additional treaty ports combined with the start of railway operations must have lowered the cost of inland transport on the one hand and facilitated access to foreign markets on the other. In an area such as this, where inland waterways provide only limited means of transport during part of the year and where highways and other forms of road transport are quite underdeveloped, railroads can become a most significant source of "social savings." There are strong indications that railroad development in Manchuria opened access to large tracts of unsettled land. It would seem that as a result, these changes in transport and communication dramatically accelerated the pace of land settlement and the rate of export growth. Some of these trends will be more clearly spelled out below.

Population

There are no systematic population series for this first phase of Manchuria's economic development, although annual population data were published by the S.M.R. research department for the 1920s. These were estimates for the three provinces of Liaoning, Kirin, and Heilungkiang, starting

---

[8] S. H. Chou, "Railway," p. 63.
[9] Bank of Chosen, *The Economic History of Manchuria*, pp. 204-5.

with a chosen year-base and an assumed annual growth rate.[10] After the establishment of the State of Manchukuo and beginning in 1932, annual population data were compiled from police registers. A close study of these data indicates that there are many discrepancies and peculiarities, so that they cannot be used, at least not in their original form.

Table 1

ESTIMATED LONG-TERM POPULATION TRENDS
IN MANCHURIA, 1860-1940

Year	Population (in thousands)*
1860	3,283
1872	4,454
1887	5,150
1898	6,943
1908	17,055
1910	17,942
1914	19,652
1930	31,300
1940	38,400

* The totals for 1860 to 1914 are based on separate estimates for each province derived from the following sources: Yen Chung-p'ing et al., *Chung-kuo chin-tai-shih t'ung-chi tz'u-liao* [Statistical materials on modern China] (Peking, 1957), pp. 362-74; Chang P'o-ying, *Heilungkiang chih-kao* [Draft gazetteer of Heilungkiang Province] (1933; facsimile reproduction, Taipei, 1965), vol. 2, p. 1181; Nakano Jiro, trans., *Manshu tsushi* [General history of Manchuria], translated from a publication of that title originally published by the Russian Ministry of Finance, ca. 1900 (Tokyo, 1906); East Asiatic Investigation Bureau, *Manchuria Year Book, 1931* (Tokyo, 1932), pp. 5-6. For 1930 and 1940, our figures are based on Manchurian totals (rather than on provincial estimates) as estimated in section A and adjusted to 1910 boundaries.

A point of departure for a systematic study of Manchurian population is provided by the census of 1940, which was conducted with great care and the results of which seem quite reliable.[11] For the nineteenth and early twentieth

---

[10] S.M.R., *Mantetsu chosa geppo* [Monthly surveys] (Dairen, November 1932), p. 19; and S.M.R., *Manshu sangyo tokei* [Manchurian industrial statistics] (Dairen, 1931), p. 7.

[11] For a detailed discussion of population data and the population census see our section A and the monograph by Walter Wynne, *The Population of*

century there are only scattered data, partly based on Ch'ing and Republican registers and partly based on Japanese sources. However, some of these estimates were derived from systematic studies of the available data and can be fitted into a reasonably plausible series for certain benchmark years as shown in table 1. In this connection, too, the 1940 census serves as a useful reference point. The data in table 1 refer to the original provinces of Manchuria, Liaoning, Kirin, and Heilungkiang. They exclude Jehol and represent an adjustment of all data to the region's 1910 boundaries.

Bearing in mind that these data may be subject to sizable margins of error, it would seem that Manchurian population may have grown from around 3 million in 1850 to 18 million around 1910 and close to 40 million by 1940. The estimates in table 1 would suggest close to a twelvefold rise in numbers in 80 years, which is an average annual growth rate of about 3.1 percent—certainly a high rate by most standards.

There is clearly a sharp discontinuity in this series between 1898 and 1908. It is most improbable that population would have increased two and one-half times in a decade. Therefore, most probably part of this increase is statistical rather than real, reflecting a considerable underestimate and undercount of population before that date. However, irrespective of this, population growth almost certainly was accelerated under the impact of railroad construction and the opening of the Chinese Eastern and South Manchurian railways.

Unfortunately, there are no systematic migration data for the nineteenth century or the first two decades of the twentieth. Therefore, we cannot determine what share of population growth was contributed by natural increases as compared to net immigration. However, we have derived annual net immigration estimates for 1924 to 1941 and have also estimated total population increase for each of these years.[12] These would suggest that close to half of the population gain for the 1924 to 1941 period as a whole can be attributed to net immigration. Naturally there were marked fluctuations in the rates of migration year by year, depending on economic and political conditions in Manchuria and in North China, whence most of the immigrants came. But for the period as a whole, immigration clearly was a major factor in defining the rate of population growth and the characteristics of this population.

Based on the 1940 census, birth rates were around 37 per thousand with death rates about 25 per thousand. This would suggest rates of natural increase of around 1.2 percent per year in the 1930s. It is unlikely that birth rates were much higher in the nineteenth century, because of a highly adverse sex ratio. In 1940, this ratio was 123.9; it may be expected that it was probably even

---

Manchuria, Bureau of the Census, International Population Reports, P-90, no. 7 (Washington, D.C., 1958).
[12] Based on section A.

higher before 1900 or 1910, when the total population was much smaller and the share of the immigrant population correspondingly larger. It is even more improbable that death rates could have been lower in the nineteenth century than around 1940. If this reasoning has any validity, rates of natural increase could not have been much higher in the late 1800s than in the 1930s. Therefore, one may surmise that immigration must have contributed even more decisively to population growth between 1860 and 1910 than during the following decades. It is possible that perhaps as much as two thirds of the population increase in Manchuria was derived from immigration during the second half of the nineteenth century. This can be considered both as a symptom of the region's rapid economic growth and one of the major sources of this growth during this period.

Cultivated Land

The most systematic compilations of land and population in China thus far are those by Dwight Perkins. We used these as a point of departure for our estimates, but supplemented them with data for Heilungkiang for the early years and added some years so as to obtain a somewhat more continuous series.

It would seem that cultivated acreage and population grew at roughly the same rate between 1872 and 1940, but the same does not hold for intermediate periods. As a result, cultivated land per capita appeared to be the same at the beginning and at the end of the period, but not for the years in between. On the other hand, if one starts the analysis in 1887, the land-man ratio exhibits a distinct downward trend. This accords with ones expectations, given the fact that cultivable land was relatively more abundant in the nineteenth than in the twentieth century. On this basis one would expect the ratio in 1872 to be higher than in 1940. To the extent that this may have been the case, the acreage figures for 1872 must have been underestimated.

Just as with population, the cultivated acreage figures for the period before and after 1908 are not comparable. Almost certainly both are underestimated for the early years, although on the basis of our reasoning above this would be more pronounced for land than for population. At the same time, one would expect a significant acceleration in the rate of growth for both between 1898 and 1908 under the impact of railroad construction and railroad operation, which opened new lands and speeded up the process of land settlement.

A declining trend in land-man ratios would also accord with the long-term historical trend in China Proper, where, as brought out by Perkins, population grew faster than area under cultivation. The resulting decline in acreage per capita was then compensated for by greatly intensified land use. Given the relatively greater abundance of land and the much more recent settlement of Manchuria, population pressure and intensity of land use was much less pronounced in this frontier region than in the rest of China. As a result, even in the 1930s and 1940s there was more than twice as much cultivated land available per capita in Manchuria than in China Proper.[13]

Table 2

ESTIMATED CULTIVATED ACREAGE AND POPULATION
TRENDS IN MANCHURIA, 1873-1930

Year	Population (in thousands)	Area (in thousand hectares)	Rates of growth (in % per year) Population	Area	Cultivated land area per capita (in hectares)
1872-73	4,454	1,752.3			0.39
			0.8	3.0	
1887	5,150	2,698.7			0.52
			5.8	5.0	
1908	17,055	7,528.9			0.44
			2.4	4.0	
1914	19,652	9,501.0			0.48
			3.0	1.8	
1930	31,300	12,576.0			0.40
			2.1	2.0	
1940	38,400	15,251.0			0.39

Sources: Dwight Perkins, Agricultural Development in China, 1368-1968 (Chicago, 1969), table B.14, p. 236. Otake Fumio, Kinse Shina keizaishi [Studies on the economic history of modern China] (Tokyo, 1942), p. 218. Wang Shu-nan et al., comps., Feng-t'ien t'ung-chih [Gazetteer of Fengtien (also known as Liaoning Province)] (Shenyang, 1934), vol. 108. Chang Sun, ed., Kirin t'ung-chih [Kirin Province gazetteer] (1930; facsimile reproduction, Taipei, 1965), vol. 4, pp. 2219-34. South Manchurian Railway Company, Hokuman keizai chosa shiryo [North Manchurian economic investigation materials] (Dairen, 1910), pp. 3-4. Chang P'o-ying, Heilungkiang t'ung-chih, vol. 2, pp. 773-890. Hsu Shih-ch'ang, comp., T'ung-san-sheng cheng-lueh [The administration of the three northeastern provinces] (Shenyang, 1911; facsimile reproduction, Taipei, 1965). Li Wen-chih et al., Chung-kuo chin-tai-shih t'ung-chi tzu-liao hsuan-chi [Selection of statistical materials on modern Chinese history] (Peking, 1957), vol. 1, pp. 60-63. Chen Nai-ruenn, Agricultural Statistics for Manchuria, 1914-1957, Cornell University, Department of Economics Working Paper no. 15, appendix table C (mimeo).

---

[13] Based on Perkin's data in Agricultural Development in China, table A.5, p. 212, and table B.14, p. 236. The land-man ratios for China Proper were 0.56 in 1873 and 0.44 in 1933, as compared to about 1.0 acres for Manchuria.

Exports

Manchurian exports rose at a most rapid rate throughout this period, exceeding by a considerable margin the rates of growth in cultivated land and population. Between 1872 and 1899, Manchurian sales abroad, including shipments to China Proper, increased at a rate of 7.1 percent a year, as may be seen from the data in table 3. The pace of export growth was significantly accelerated after 1907, when the C.E.R. and S.M.R. were fully operational and the Port of Dairen was opened as well. They rose to 11 percent per year for the 1907 to 1929 period.

Strictly speaking, the series for the years before and after 1907 as given in appendix table I are not comparable. The data for 1872 to 1907 refer to export shipments only through the port of Newchwang. However, in the absence of railways and other seaports, the bulk of exports moved through this port during that period. Undoubtedly some goods moved overland to North China, but they could not have been significant enough and variable enough to affect the rate of growth appreciably. In 1907 additional ports were opened and exports were now also carried overland by rail.

Table 3

FOREIGN TRADE OF MANCHURIA, 1872-1929

(in million yuan)

Year	Imports Current prices	1913 prices	Exports Current prices	1913 prices	Total Current prices	1913 prices
1872	5.3	11.5	3.1	6.4	8.4	17.9
1899	43.2	64.3	32.1	41.2	75.3	105.5
1905	77.5	95.4	18.7	20.7	96.2	116.1
1907	55.3	67.2	38.0	38.9	93.3	106.1
1909	123.1	117.1	141.6	128.1	264.7	245.2
1929	513.5	324.8	663.1	390.5	1,176.6	715.3

Sources: Appendix tables I and II.

Manchuria's principal export staples were soybeans, bean cake, and bean oil, which constituted 87 percent of total sales in 1872. However, the share of this staple in the region's export shipments declined gradually and consistently; it was 81 percent in 1899 and 60 percent in 1929. This declining share was a result of the fact that bean exports increased more slowly than total exports. This tendency was particularly pronounced in the 1907 or 1909 to 1929 period, with the former growing at the 5.3 percent rate, while the latter rose at an annual average of 11 percent.

The declining share of soybean exports, coupled with very rapid export expansion, serves as an indication of the growing diversification of the Manchurian economy. At the same time, the fact that total exports, and even soybean shipments, outpaced the rise in population suggests the possibility that national product per capita may have been rising quite appreciably between 1872 and 1929. This, of course, is based on the assumption that, to some extent at least, export expansion may serve as a proxy for national product growth. The divergence between population increases and export growth is so significant that even if exports rose more rapidly than domestic product, there would still be room left for a rise in per capita product.

Table 4

EXPORTS OF SOYBEANS AND SOYBEAN PRODUCTS
FROM MANCHURIA, 1867-1929

| Year | Export value (in million yuan) | |
	in current prices	in 1934 prices
1867	n.a.	7.7
1872	2.7	6.9
1891	10.2	24.8
1899	26.0	31.0
1905	14.2	10.3
1909*		91.0
1915		107.3
1929	397.9	255.5

* There is a sharp discontinuity between the series prior to 1907 and thereafter relating to differences in coverage.

Source: Appendix table III.

A Recapitulation

In this section, we have tried to throw some light on the rate and pattern of development based on very scanty data between 1860 and 1930. It seems to us that this is a case study of extensive growth in a newly settled region in which economic development is dependent on a rapid expansion of inputs. At the same time, it is a case which seems to be reasonably well explained by the staple theory of growth.

Watkins identifies two distinct traits in the initial conditions charac-terizing economic development of newly settled countries or regions: a favorable man-land ratio and an absence of inhibiting traditions.[14] These initial conditions prevailed in Manchuria in the latter part of the nineteenth century, at least as compared to China Proper and other economies in East and Southeast Asia. He then points out that from these initial features flow some probable consequences for the growth process, at least in the early phases; staple exports are the leading sector, setting the pace for economic growth, and the import of scarce factors of production is essential. Moreover, growth, if it is to be stable, requires an ability to shift resources that may be hindered by excessive reliance on exports in general and, in particular, on a small number of staple exports.

These conditions are met in the Manchurian case. Economic growth was propelled by the mutual interaction of population growth, expansion in culti-vated acreage, and the rapid rise in staple exports. Population supplied one of the key inputs, labor, which in combination with land provided the wherewithal for increasing agricultural production. This rising production, in turn, provided for the consumption needs of a rapidly increasing population and supplied staple exports to foreign markets. The demand forces generated by population and export growth stimulated a further expansion in output, which, in turn, fostered the demand for additional inputs of land and labor. In this way, a mechanism was created for an ongoing process of economic development.

The process was crucially dependent on the importation of labor and cap-ital on the one hand and the export of soybeans and soybean products on the other. Unskilled and farm labor were imported from China, while managerial and technical skills, together with capital, were imported from Russia and later predominantly from Japan. Most of the imported capital and skill was initially devoted to railroad construction and operation, which served to reinforce and broaden the growth process referred to above. Second, it went into the development of trade and services associated with railroad development. As the economy became more advanced and somewhat more complex, soybeans and soybean products declined in importance and exports became more diversified. Gradually, and especially beginning in the 1920s, industrial development began to gain momentum, so that the economy was becoming less dependent on exports in general and soybean shipments in particular. This tendency became even more pronounced in the 1930s, as will be documented in greater detail in the next section of this paper.

Industrial Development in the Interwar Period, 1924-41

It would seem that the period of extensive growth based on an expansion of the agricultural frontier was largely ended around 1930. This is quite clearly

---

[14] Melville H. Watkins, "A Stable Theory of Growth," *Canadian Journal of Economics and Political Science* 29 (May 1963).

evidenced by the fact that total grain output—based on annual figures for 1924 to 1941—attained its peak level in 1930, and the three-year crop production average for 1929-31 was perceptibly higher than for 1939-41.[15]

This development was paralleled by a slowdown in export growth, coupled with a rapid rise in commodity imports and growing trade deficits financed by capital imports, mostly from Japan. At an earlier stage, capital imports were largely channeled into railroad development, which contributed to agricultural expansion and rising exports. By 1930 or so, most of the more fertile lands were under cultivation and further agricultural growth became increasingly dependent on rising input productivity requiring investment of capital and technological progress. However, the Japanese, who increasingly dominated economic policy direction in Manchuria, chose instead to concentrate on industrial development, on further extension of the railroad network for strategic and industrial development reasons, and on the development of commerce and government services.

These findings can be much more firmly documented than those for the preceding period, since beginning in the 1920s much more detailed and systematic statistics began to be collected and published in Manchuria. On the basis of these statistics it became possible to construct a series of national product estimates for certain years between 1924 and 1941. Our analysis of economic growth and structural transformation is based on these detailed sectoral estimates, which will be published when our study as a whole is complete.

The data are generally better for the 1930s than for the 1920s, and therefore our estimates for 1934-41 are more reliable than those for 1924-29. Many statistical problems were encountered in the process of constructing the estimates, and often circuitous and indirect approaches had to be resorted to in order to resolve particular problems. Yet, it seems to us that on balance these are reasonably reliable and usable estimates. Great care was taken by us to make these estimates territorially comparable. Thus they refer to all the four northeastern provinces, the Kwantung Leased Territory and the SMR Zone.[16]

---

[15] These annual crop data are presented in section C. These in turn are based on the following three sources: *Manshu kaihatsu yonjunenshi* [The history of forty years development in Manchuria] (Tokyo: Manshikai, 1964); *Tung-pei nien-chien, 1931* [The yearbook of the Northeast, 1931] (Mukden: Tungpei Culture Press, 1932); S.M.R., *Manshu nosan tokei* [Agricultural statistics of Manchuria] (Dairen, 1943).

[16] The Kwantung Territory, situated on the tip of the eastern Liaoning Peninsula, was leased by Japan from China when the Russo-Japanese War ended. It encompasses an area of 3,462 square kilometers. At the same time, the Japanese acquired the right to administer the lands on both sides of the South Manchurian Railway [here called the SMR Zone], a total area of 298 square kilometers.

This means that our territorial coverage for this period not only refers to Liaoning, Kirin, and Heilungkiang, but to Jehol as well.

The Rate of Growth

Bearing these qualifications in mind, as may be seen from table 5, the average annual rate of growth in the Manchurian economy was about 4 percent a year for the 1924-41 period. This is clearly a high rate by pre-World War II standards. The most rapidly growing sectors were construction, factory indus-try, and modern transport, and the periods of most rapid growth were between 1924 and 1929 and, particularly, 1936-41. On the other hand, growth was quite slow between 1929 and 1936 due to the sluggishness of agricultural production, associated with the Mukden Incident and the formation of the new "State of Manchukuo," and the impact of the world depression. Actually, the growth rates for 1924-34 and 1929-34 illustrate the sharp drop in farm output, which reached its low for the period in 1934. What is also evident from these figures is that in the 1920s, agriculture was still a dynamic sector, significantly contributing to economic growth, while from 1929 on it experienced very slow growth.

Table 5

GROSS DOMESTIC PRODUCT OF MANCHURIA, 1924-41
AVERAGE ANNUAL RATES *(percentages)*

	1924-29	1929-34	1924-34	1929-36	1924-36	1936-41	1924-41
A sector*	5.3	-8.5	-1.8	0.9	1.6	2.4	1.9
M sector	3.1	5.8	4.3	5.5	4.4	9.9	6.0
S sector	5.1	2.1	3.3	2.6	3.6	10.5	5.6
A and M sectors	4.8	-4.5	-0.7	-0.7	2.4	4.9	3.1
Transportation and trade	5.8	3.1	4.4	3.3	4.2	7.8	5.3
TOTAL GDP	**4.9**	**-2.0**	**1.3**	**1.4**	**2.8**	**7.3**	**4.2**

* The "A sector" includes farm production, processing activities in agriculture, forestry, and fishing; the "M sector" refers to mining, manufacturing, public utilities, small-scale industry, and construction; all other economic activities are encompassed under the "S sector."

Sources: Sections A-O; the raw material for these sections and the data on which they are based were for the most part culled from the archives and research library of the South Manchurian Railway Company deposited in the Library of Congress.

Table 6

PER CAPITA GDP IN MANCHURIA, 1924-41

(in 1934 yuan)

Year	Population* (1)	GDP (in millions) (2)	Per capita GDP (3)
1924	31,030,000	2,348.0	75.7
1926	32,477,000	2,639.3	81.3
1929	35,759,000	2,986.4	83.5
1934	38,668,000	2,677.1	69.2
1936	39,984,000	3,289.6	82.3
1939	43,035,000	4,174.8	97.0
1941	45,755,000	4,733.3	103.4

* These population series are not comparable with those in tables 1 and 2, since the former are based on three northeastern provinces, i.e., they exclude Jehol, while the present do not.

Sources: Col. (1): Section A. Col. (2): Sections C-O. Col. (3): Derived from cols. (1) and (2).

The position of manufacturing was almost the reverse of agriculture: it expanded rather slowly in the 1920s, but was a most dynamic sector in the 1930s, especially from the mid-thirties on, when the industrialization program of the new puppet state gained full momentum under Japanese tutelage. Another notable feature of Manchuria's growth pattern is the rapid expansion of the service sector. This was particularly pronounced in the 1936-41 period and may in part be ascribed to the construction of a large apparatus for the new "state." As a result, government services rose at 17 percent per year during these five years. Modern transportation was another very dynamic sector, largely due to the rapid growth of railway traffic.

As was indicated in the preceding section, Manchurian development was characterized by marked increases in population. During the years under consideration here, population increased at an estimated average annual rate of 2.3 percent. This means that domestic product per capita rose at a rate of close to 2 percent a year.

This, too, is quite a high rate by pre-World War II standards of presently industrialized countries. Two percent a year per capita rates of growth in national product were attained or exceeded in the process of their industrialization of Sweden and Japan. However, for some periods such rates were also attained in Great Britain, Denmark, the U.S., and Canada.[17]

---

[17] Based on Simon Kuznets's *Economic Growth of Nations: Total Output and Production Structure* (Cambridge, Mass.: Harvard University Press, 1971), table 4, pp. 38-40.

Moreover, high rates of per capita growth—significantly in excess of the long-term historical rates—have been attained in a number of countries since World War II, including many underdeveloped countries. Finally, while fairly high rates of per capita growth characterized Manchurian development, almost certainly this was not the case in China Proper.[18]

Table 7

INTERSECTORAL COMPOSITION OF GDP IN MANCHURIA, 1924-41
(in percent and based on 1934 yuan)

	1924	1926	1928	1934	1936	1939	1941
Agriculture	44.7	45.7	45.7	32.2	38.5	29.2	29.4
Subsidiary production of agriculture	4.0	4.1	4.1	2.9	3.4	2.6	2.6
Fishing	0.2	0.2	0.4	0.5	0.5	0.5	0.4
Forestry	0.8	0.5	0.5	0.6	0.8	1.4	1.5
Mining	1.4	1.6	1.4	1.7	2.1	2.4	2.6
Factory industry	2.3	2.7	2.8	3.8	5.1	7.9	7.6
Small-scale industry	9.8	8.7	7.7	8.9	7.0	4.4	4.7
Construction	1.2	0.8	1.0	5.4	3.5	5.7	5.4
Modern transport and communications	3.5	3.5	3.7	4.9	4.5	6.9	7.6
Traditional transport	0.8	0.8	0.9	1.1	1.0	1.0	1.0
Trade	15.7	15.7	16.2	21.1	18.2	17.0	15.8
Government and other services	10.0	10.0	10.0	11.2	9.7	15.2	15.9
Housing services	5.7	5.7	5.7	5.7	5.7	5.7	5.7

Table 7a

(in percent and based on 1934 yuan)

	1924	1926	1929	1934	1936	1939	1941
A+	49.7	50.1	50.7	36.2	43.2	32.7	33.9
M+	14.7	16.8	12.9	19.8	17.7	20.4	20.3
S	35.6	33.1	36.4	44.0	39.1	46.9	45.8

Sources: Sections C-O.

---

[18] There are detailed GNP estimates for China only for 1933. There are more skeletal estimates for 1931-36, but none for a longer time span. Therefore, no firm quantitative statements are possible, but all of the qualitative evidence would speak against a sustained rise in per capita product between 1920 and 1940.

Changes in Economic Structure

This rapid growth necessarily entailed a marked transformation in the structure of the economy, as may be seen from tables 7 and 7A. It resulted in a significant decline in the relative importance of the agricultural sector from one-half to one-third of GDP, paralleled by a rise in the M+ sector from about 15 to 20 percent and in the S sector from 35 to 45 percent. Agriculture remained throughout the single most important sector, followed by trade and government and other services. Despite rapid industrial development, manufacturing did not change its relative importance throughout; factory industry grew at the expense of small-scale industry, but industry as a whole expanded at the same rate as GDP, thus not gaining in relative importance. One of the most striking characteristics of the development pattern exhibited by table 7 is the increasing service orientation of the Manchurian economy. Service activities gained in relative importance at the expense of commodity production.

Another way of assessing Manchuria's economic progress and transformation is to compare its economic structure with that of other countries at differing stages of development. Using Simon Kuznets's classification as the standard, the Manchurian economy of 1924 would most closely approximate the lowest category, with per capita incomes of about $52 in terms of 1958 dollars. However, Manchuria's S share was much larger than that associated with the poorest countries; therefore, by the standards of that sector it would belong to Category III.[19]

By 1941 the Manchurian economy had clearly moved up in the international development scale, but in a peculiarly "unbalanced" fashion. Its agricultural sector share would have placed it in Category IV, its M share, however, left it in Category I, and its S share placed it in the highest category or above. The change in Manchuria's position on this S-share scale can be wholly attributed to relative gains in modern transport and government services. At the same time, while the trade share in GDP did not change very much between 1924 and 1941, it also placed Manchuria near the top of the scale, while in terms of per capita income level it certainly was close to the lower end. This may be a function of Manchuria's strong foreign trade orientation, with an export share of about 17 percent and an import share of 22 percent in relation to 1934 GDP.[20] At the same time it reflects an inflation of government services to supply the region with the attributes of statehood and to develop a bureaucracy for administering wartime controls.

---

[19] See Simon Kuznets, *Economic Growth of Nations*, table 12, p. 104, with sectors I and S adjusted to our definitions, i.e., transport and communications transferred from I to S.

[20] Based on foreign trade data in appendix table I and our GDP estimates.

These peculiarities in Manchuria's economic structure were by no means unprecedented, as may be illustrated by the data in table 8. The U.S. in 1839 had a higher per capita product (in comparable dollars) than Manchuria in 1924 or 1941. In terms of economic structure, however, it did not differ radically from the Manchurian one in 1924, although its A and S sectors were somewhat smaller, while its M sector was larger. On the other hand, Australia—another newly settled region—was by the 1860s more advanced than Manchuria in the interwar period, both in terms of per capita product and economic structure.

Table 8

INTERSECTORAL COMPOSITION OF GROSS DOMESTIC PRODUCT
IN SELECTED COUNTRIES

	A	M	S
United States			
1839	42.6	24.5	32.9
1889-99	17.9	40.5	41.6
Australia, 1861-70	25.1	30.0	44.9
Sweden, 1861-70	38.3	21.0	40.7
Brazil, 1960	28.2	25.8	46.0
Burma,1960	31.8	17.8	50.4
Ceylon, 1960	47.8	12.2	40.0
Malaysia, 1960	37.8	18.9	43.3
Thailand, 1960	37.4	17.7	44.9
Taiwan, 1960	33.4	26.9	39.7
Pakistan, 1960	53.5	12.1	34.4
India, 1960*	48.6	18.3	33.1

* Net domestic product.

Sources: Simon Kuznets, *Economic Growth of Nations,* tables 21 and 22, p. 147, and pp. 160-162; and United Nations, *Yearbook of National Accounts Statistics, 1965* (New York, 1966).

In comparison with another relatively "new" but less developed country than the U.S. or Australia (Brazil, for example), Manchuria's position would not seem at all anomalous. This conclusion is reinforced in comparison with a number of Asian countries of the post-World War II period. In all of these the S sector looms relatively large. For instance, Burma in 1960 had a somewhat smaller A and M sector than Manchuria in 1941, but a larger S sector. In contrast, Taiwan (1960) and Manchuria (1941) had about the same size A sector, but the former was more industrialized and correspondingly less service-oriented than the latter.

Comparative Growth Patterns in China and Manchuria

As noted earlier, rapid growth and economic transformation in Manchuria led to a marked increase in per capita product. In the meantime, there is no evidence of a comparable expansion in China, so that during the interwar period the Manchurian and Chinese economies were following clearly divergent paths. If we compare the single prewar year for which there are detailed national product estimates for China, 1933, with our 1934 estimates for Manchuria, the lag in the stage of development of the former as compared to the latter is demonstrated once more. The contrast would undoubtedly be even greater if we could separate out Manchuria from the all-China estimates and in this way obtain comparisons for China Proper and Manchuria. The divergence between the two increased in time, in part due to the fact that industrialization and economic development continued in Manchuria even after the outbreak of the Sino-Japanese War in 1937, while it was halted or set back drastically in the rest of China.

The Chinese economy more or less recovered from the impact of war and civil war by 1952; therefore we chose this year for comparison with Manchuria in 1941. This is based on the presupposition that in the absence of the Sino-Japanese War the Chinese economy might in some sense have attained its 1952 level by 1941.

Proceeding on this basis and in terms of 1933 prices for China and 1934 prices for Manchuria, the comparative per capita product of the two is as follows (in yuan):[21]

	1930s	1940s
Manchuria	69.2 [1934]	103.4 [1941]
China	59.4 [1933]	59.3 [1952]

As may be seen from these figures, Manchurian per capita product exceeded the Chinese level by 16 percent in the early 1930s. This almost certainly understates the difference between the two, since 1934 was a particularly poor harvest year in Manchuria. As may be seen from table 6, if we compare 1929 or 1936 product with China's in 1933, the difference between the two per capita products would not be 16, but close to 40 percent. By 1941, as compared to China in 1952, this divergence rose to about 75 percent. However, this difference may be overstated by the way Chinese product was estimated for 1952.[22]

---

[21] The Manchurian estimates are based on table 6 of this paper. Those for China are from T. C. Liu and K. C. Yeh, *The Economy of the Chinese Mainland, National Income and Economic Development, 1933-59* (Princeton: Princeton University Press, 1965), tables 8 and 51.

[22] The agricultural product estimates by Liu and Yeh for 1952 are based on certain assumptions which yield a definite downward bias.

These differences in the respective levels of development are also reflected in the structures of the two economies, as may be seen from table 9. By the 1930s, Manchuria's economy was less agricultural, more industrial, and more service-oriented than China's. These differences persisted into the later period, but they were narrowed somewhat, as the Chinese economy of 1952 was more developed than that of 1933.

Table 9

GROSS DOMESTIC PRODUCT BY INDUSTRIAL ORIGIN
IN CHINA AND MANCHURIA
(in percent)

	China (in 1933 prices)		Manchuria (in 1934 prices)	
	1933	*1952*	*1934*	*1941*
A	65.0	56.6	36.0	33.9
M	11.5	14.5	19.7	20.3
S	23.5	28.9	44.3	45.8

Sources: Table 7a of this paper; Liu and Yeh, *Economy*, table 8.

The divergent development paths of China and Manchuria are not at all surprising, given the course the two economies have followed within the past century. Another basic symptom of these differences as well as a major factor contributing to them is the investment rate. Thus the rate of gross investment in fixed capital was 9 percent in Manchuria by 1924, over 17 percent in 1934, and 23 percent in 1939. In contrast, the corresponding rate in China was only around 5 percent in 1933 and the high Manchurian rates were not attained in the country as a whole until the end of the First Five-Year Plan, around 1956 to 1957.[23] The high prewar investment levels attained in Manchuria in the late 1930s were to a large extent financed by capital imports from Japan.

Under the impact of this rapid development, how significant an asset did Manchuria represent to the Chinese economy as a whole? In the early 1930s, about 8 percent of China's population lived in the northeast and this rose to 9 percent by 1952. If we compare 1941 outputs in Manchuria with those of China in 1952 (in comparable prices), it would seem that the region contributed about

---

[23] Rates for China based on Liu and Yeh, *Economy*, table 71, and on Kang Chao's *Capital Formation in China, 1952-1965*, manuscript to be published by the University of California Press, table 10; rates for Manchuria are from section A.

14 percent of the country's national product, almost a third to its factory product, and over 43 percent to the value added by modern transport.[24] The scattered and partial evidence thus far available would suggest that by 1952, Manchurian production had not yet fully recovered to pre-1949 peak levels, but, on the average, 1941 and 1952 outputs for the region may be roughly comparable.

Assuming that this was the case, the Japanese clearly left behind them a most important economic legacy when they surrendered Manchuria in 1945. They left a much more developed region than they acquired and one that would make a major contribution to the industrialization and economic development of a revitalized China.

Alexander Eckstein, University of Michigan
Kang Chao, University of Wisconsin
John Chang, Asian Development Bank

---

[24] Based on a comparison of our total GDP and sectoral estimates for 1941 (in 1934 prices) with those for China in 1952 (in 1933 prices) as derived by us from Liu and Yeh, *Economy*, table 8.

Appendix Table I

FOREIGN TRADE OF MANCHURIA, 1872-1941
(in million yuan)

Year	Imports	Exports	Total
1872	5.3	3.1	8.4
1873	4.9	2.5	7.4
1874	3.8	2.7	6.5
1875	4.4	4.2	8.6
1876	6.7	4.1	10.8
1877	5.8	4.9	10.7
1878	8.4	6.8	15.2
1879	7.1	5.7	12.8
1880	5.3	5.2	10.8
1881	3.9	5.5	9.4
1882	4.7	5.6	10.3
1883	4.8	6.1	10.9
1884	5.7	6.4	12.1
1885	5.8	7.1	12.9
1886	6.3	7.0	13.3
1887	7.6	8.5	16.1
1888	6.7	8.9	15.6
1889	6.0	8.7	14.7
1890	11.3	11.2	22.5
1891	14.0	12.6	26.6
1892	11.4	14.1	25.5
1893	13.0	14.5	27.5
1894	12.3	13.3	25.6
1895	5.8	8.7	14.5
1896	17.9	17.6	35.5
1897	19.6	21.5	41.1
1898	23.4	27.2	50.6
1899	43.2	32.1	75.3
1900	16.4	18.0	34.4
1901	36.6	29.2	65.8
1902	39.2	27.3	66.5
1903	43.1	31.1	74.2
1904	45.7	18.9	64.6
1905	77.5	18.7	96.2
1906	46.3	23.0	69.3
1907	25.8	24.5	50.3

Year	Imports	Exports	Total
1907*	55.3	38.0	93.3
1908	93.9	85.8	179.7
1909	123.1	141.6	264.7
1910	138.4	145.7	284.1
1911	161.9	169.8	331.7
1912	165.5	160.9	326.4
1913	174.5	177.4	351.9
1914	175.1	169.7	344.8
1915	168.4	202.7	371.1
1916	201.8	203.8	405.6
1917	247.1	251.0	498.1
1918	276.1	259.9	536.0
1919	360.4	352.0	712.4
1920	319.5	367.5	687.0
1921	340.0	365.2	705.2
1922	306.0	427.8	733.8
1923	322.5	457.9	780.4
1924	312.5	419.0	731.5
1925	381.2	486.7	867.9
1926	431.3	577.6	1,008.9
1927	418.9	635.6	1,054.5
1928	471.9	676.2	1,148.1
1929	513.5	663.1	1,176.6
1930	478.3	618.1	1,096.4
1931	341.0	722.8	1,063.8
1932	337.7	618.2	955.9
1933	515.8	448.5	964.3
1934	593.6	448.4	1,042.0
1935	604.1	421.1	1,025.2
1936	691.8	602.8	1,294.6
1937	887.4	645.3	1,532.7
1938	1,274.7	725.5	2,000.2
1939	1,783.4	826.2	2,609.6
1940	1,563.3	572.5	2,135.8
1941	1,260.9	608.8	1,869.7

* Series before and after 1907 not comparable. See text.

Sources: Bank of Chosen, Economic History of Manchuria (Seoul, 1920), pp. 21-22; The Manchukuo Yearbook, 1934; S.M.R., "The Foreign Trade of Manchukuo Since Its Inception," Contemporary Manchuria 3 (April 1939) and 4 (July 1939).

Appendix Table II

INDEX NUMBERS OF PRICES OF IMPORTS AND EXPORTS
(1913 = 100)

Year	Imports	Exports
1872	45.8	48.7
1899	67.2	78.0
1905	81.2	90.4
1907	82.3	97.6
1909	95.1	90.5
1929	158.1	169.8

Source: Nankai Institute of Economics, Nankai Index Numbers, 1936 (Tientsin, 1937), table VII, pp. 37–38.

Appendix Table III

EXPORTS OF SOYBEANS, BEAN CAKE, AND BEAN OIL, 1867–1938

Year	Quantity (in thousand short tons)			Value (in thousands)		
	Soybeans (1)	Bean cake (2)	Bean oil (3)	HKT (4)	Yuan (5)	1934 yuan (6)
1867	76.1	81.4	1.5			7,741
1868	53.9	41.1	.9			4,831
1869	97.8	61.5	2.3			8,372
1870	64.9	51.3	9.0			7,085
1871	64.9	27.1	.9			4,940
1872	82.4	43.9	2.8	1,738	2,711	6,884
1873	67.0	36.9	1.3	1,252	1,953	5,495
1874	73.5	50.6	1.7	1,372	2,140	6,454
1875	116.0	67.1	.8	2,214	3,454	9,415
1876	94.7	50.7	.3	2,088	3,257	7,479
1877	95.9	52.8	.3	2,388	3,725	7,628
1878	143.7	128.3	.2	3,509	5,474	13,256
1879	123.5	120.1	.8	3,151	4,916	11,861
1880	141.4	90.1	1.8	2,718	4,240	11,917
1881	150.7	96.2	1.5	2,801	4,370	12,644
1882	137.9	107.5	1.4	2,961	4,619	12,312
1883	156.2	114.4	1.1	3,241	5,058	13,593
1884	140.1	125.1	1.4	3,281	5,118	13,107

Year	Quantity (in thousand short tons)			Value (in thousands)		
	Soybeans (1)	Bean cake (2)	Bean oil (3)	HKT (4)	Yuan (5)	1934 yuan (6)
1885	170.8	120.3	.7	3,576	5,579	14,606
1886	126.6	98.7	.1	3,136	4,892	11,124
1887	173.1	135.4	2.3	4,007	6,251	15,555
1888	176.7	124.3	.9	4,357	6,797	15,131
1889	127.8	126.2	3.8	3,987	6,220	12,797
1890	187.4	174.9	2.1	5,070	7,909	17,854
1891	277.2	204.3	6.2	6,563	10,238	24,816
1892	278.0	187.9	8.1	6,495	10,132	24,529
1893	222.7	155.1	5.9	7,065	11,021	19,734
1894	249.1	177.3	4.9	6,676	10,415	21,960
1895	196.7	52.8	2.2	4,579	7,143	13,783
1896	255.7	181.6	5.9	9,455	14,750	20,913
1897	258.2	220.5	5.0	11,372	17,740	24,142
1898	281.4	246.4	7.2	14,740	22,994	26,808
1899	314.1	292.1	10.7	16,685	26,029	30,973
1900	167.9	194.1	14.9	9,643	15,043	19,387
1901	168.9	288.8	13.9	16,088	25,097	22,883
1902	228.7	309.1	18.8	14,100	21,996	27,875
1903	228.3	303.5	7.5	14,630	22,823	25,927
1904	121.7	132.4	4.8	8,750	13,650	12,829
1905	98.9	114.3	1.7	9,080	14,165	10,346
1906	137.5	244.2	6.4	11,850	18,486	18,228
1907	76.2	244.6	5.6			14,554
1909*	977.4	717.2	38.0			90,991
1910	831.5	637.8	46.1			79,555
1911	821.9	911.9	67.3			92,598
1912	650.1	727.1	58.6			74,277
1913	532.6	907.3	73.2			76,481
1914	672.4	804.8	49.1			77,079
1915	928.9	1,073.3	82.9			107,308
1916	575.6	992.6	103.5			86,810
1917	651.7	1,255.6	128.0			104,920
1918	512.2	1,332.6	152.4			103,419
1919	772.0	1,504.6	1,153.3			125,195
1920	701.1	1,500.7	138.9			118,738
1921	855.3	1,658.5	131.7			132,582

* 1867-1907 and 1909-38 series are not comparable.

	Quantity (in thousand short tons)			Value (in thousands)		
Year	Soybeans (1)	Bean cake (2)	Bean oil (3)	HKT (4)	Yuan (5)	1934 yuan (6)
1922	1,148.5	1,790.9	171.7			160,748
1923	1,322.4	2,048.3	173.1			180,836
1924	1,509.6	1,879.7	152.1			182,158
1925	1,614.1	1,747.4	168.7			185,727
1926	1,577.5	2,129.2	199.3			212,721
1927	2,034.6	2,192.3	180.6	215,955	336,890	228,881
1928	2,681.4	1,813.2	142.2	245,722	383,328	246,335
1929	3,041.9	1,548.9	130.2	255,052	397,881	255,480
1930	2,473.4	1,673.5	149.1	206,901	322,766	229,981
1931	3,126.5	2,091.7	206.6	274,233	427,803	292,558
1932	2,826.5	1,567.9	141.3	234,681	366,102	245,346
1933	2,607.4	1,185.9	89.5		245,181	210,264
1934	2,753.9	1,358.7	107.2		228,018	228,023
1935	1,946.9	1,128.3	98.6		201,555	171,020
1936	2,169.3	935.1	74.0		284,760	172,912
1937	2,242.8	884.6	77.4		310,611	175,791
1938	2,390.5	959.9	62.9		318,611	185,014

Sources: Cols. (1)–(3): 1867-1907: K. C. Sun, The Economic Development of Manchuria, p. 15; 1909-29: S.M.R., Second Report on Progress in Manchuria to 1930 (Dairen, 1931), p. 144; 1930: The Manchuria Yearbook, 1932-33 (Tokyo, 1932), pp. 342, 348, and 350; 1931-38: Manshu nenkan [Manchuria yearbook], 1932, 1936, 1937, 1939, and 1940. Col. (4): 1867-1901: Ishida Kohei, Manshu ni okeru shokuminchi keizai no shiteki tenkai [The historical development of colonial economy in Manchuria] (Kyoto: Mineruwa, 1965), table 1.20, p. 290; 1902-07: Bank of Chosen, Economic History of Manchuria (Seoul, 1920); 1927: S.M.R., Report on Progress in Manchuria, 1907-1928 (Dairen, 1929), p. 112; 1928-30: The Manchuria Yearbook, 1932-33 (Tokyo, 1932), pp. 342, 348, and 350; 1931-32: Manshu nenkan, 1932. Col. (5): HKT converted into yuan at a rate of 1.56 yuan per HKT based on Frank N. Tamagna, Banking and Finance in China (New York: Institute of Pacific Relations, 1942). Col. (6): Based on the following prices for 1934: soybeans, 58.2 yuan per short ton; bean cake, 37.9 yuan per short ton; and bean oil, 151.6 yuan per short ton. All of these prices were obtained from S.M.R., Manshu keizai tokai nempo [Annual report of Manchurian economic statistics] (Dairen, 1939), pp. 184, 190, and 191.

SECTIONS A–O

INTRODUCTION TO SECTIONS A–O

For most of the Ch'ing dynasty, Manchuria was isolated, administratively and economically, from China Proper under the frontier policy of the Manchu empire. This isolation was partially maintained during the early years of the Republic when the region was ruled by the warlord Chang Tso-lin, who was virtually independent of the Chinese central government. After the invasion by the Japanese Kwantung Army in September 1931, the region was converted into the puppet state of Manchukuo.

Through the mid-1940s, this special political situation, coupled with the area's favorable natural endowment and the forceful industrialization carried out by the Japanese-Manchukuo authorities, shaped the separate pattern of economic development in the region. Important features of this development pattern are manifested in the regional GDP statistics we have collected.

Our data are generally better for the 1930s than for the 1920s, and our estimates for 1934–41 are therefore more reliable than those for 1924–29. The Manchukuo authorities made an effort to compute national income in 1941 (see source no. [3]). After that year, however, they began to withhold economic information on the grounds of maintaining wartime security. In addition to the official national income estimates for 1941, we have gathered a large amount of economic data. Reference to these sources will be made according to the numbers assigned them in the bibliography (for example, [3] above refers to the Association of Survey Research Organizations in Manchuria).

Many statistical problems were encountered in the process of constructing the estimates, as has been noted in the article originally published in the *Journal of Economic History* that precedes these sections.

A. REGIONAL GROSS DOMESTIC PRODUCT OF MANCHURIA, 1924-41

Four main computational methods based on availability of data have been used to estimate GDP for the thirteen sectors listed in table A-1.

(1) First, for the agricultural, mining, factory industry, modern transport and communications, and traditional transport sectors, we have tried to include, as completely as possible, the output series in physical units for the commodities and services produced in each sector. The output series were converted from physical units into gross values by multiplying the figures by market prices for the goods and services. Deductible costs were then subtracted from these gross values in order to derive the value-added figures.

(2) The second method applies to the fishing, lumber, and construction sectors. The coverage of the output series for each of these sectors was incomplete. Thus, the output series must be considered as a sample indicative of the overall pattern of production in the sector. That is, we put the existing output series into an index form with 1941 as the base year (1941 = 100). These index numbers were then multiplied by the value-added figure calculated for 1941.

(3) For small workshops, trade, and government employees and other services there are no output statistics; however, some input (employment) series are available. We were compelled to use the employment series as proxies for output series. The indexes of employment (derived from the employment statistics) were then multiplied by the official value-added figure for 1941 (see section B).

(4) Subsidiary production of agriculture and residential rent are the remaining categories. For these we obtained some constant ratios to other values from sample studies and then used these ratios to derive the GDP originating from these sectors.

All resulting value-added figures, however derived, were deflated to the constant 1934 yuan, using selected price indexes as deflators. The results are summed up and presented in table A-1 and are expressed in percentages in table A-2. The per capita GDP figures are shown in table A-3. We have grouped the thirteen sectors in tables A-1 and A-2 into three composite sectors designated "A," "M," and "S," representing agriculture, mining, and services, respectively; these are indicated in the tables. Average annual rates of growth for the whole region and for each composite sector are presented in table A-4.

31

Table A-1

GROSS DOMESTIC PRODUCT OF MANCHURIA

(value-added figures in million 1934 yuan)

	1924	1926	1929	1934	1936	1939	1941
A SECTOR:							
Agriculture (C-16)	1,048.7	1,205.3	1,363.3	861.8	1,265.7	1,219.7	1,390.1
Subsidiary production of							
agriculture (D)	71.3	82.0	92.7	58.6	86.1	82.9	94.5
Fishing (E-2)	3.7	5.5	11.0	14.1	15.4	20.0	17.1
Forestry (F)	19.9	13.8	15.7	16.4	27.1	59.7	72.5
M SECTOR:							
Mining (G-4)	33.6	41.0	41.4	46.6	69.7	101.9	122.3
Factory industry (H-9)	54.0	72.3	84.5	102.8	168.3	328.1	358.0
Small workshops (I)	230.0	230.0	230.0	238.3	231.0	183.5	222.8
Construction (J-3)	89.3	91.4	115.5	143.3	113.8	238.3	253.8
S SECTOR:							
Modern transport and							
communications (K-6)	82.5	92.0	109.5	130.8	149.5	288.1	358.7
Traditional transport (L-7)	18.5	21.2	25.8	30.4	31.7	42.0	48.3
Trade (M-3)	368.0	414.3	485.2	563.6	597.4	711.8	745.6
Government employees,							
professionals, household							
services, others (N-2)	239.3	268.8	305.0	299.7	319.9	635.1	750.6
Residential rent (O-2)	133.8	150.5	170.3	152.6	187.5	238.0	296.8
TOTAL Gross							
Domestic Product	**2,392.6**	**2,688.1**	**3,049.9**	**2,659.0**	**3,263.1**	**4,149.1**	**4,731.1**

Sources: All data have been derived from sections C-O, with the following two exceptions: "small workshops" figures for 1924-29 are estimated at 230 million yuan on the basis of 1934-41 employment data; the contribution of "government employees, professionals, household services, and others" to the GDP is assumed to be 10% of the total GDP. Letters and numbers in parentheses following the category names indicate the section and table from which the figures are drawn.

Table A-2

INTERSECTORAL COMPOSITION OF GDP

[Final estimates for table 7, p. 16]

(in percent and based on 1934 yuan)

	1924	1926	1929	1934	1936	1939	1941
A SECTOR:							
Agriculture	43.8	44.8	44.7	32.4	38.8	29.4	29.6
Subsidiary production of agriculture	3.0	3.1	3.0	2.2	2.6	2.0	2.0
Fishing	0.2	0.2	0.4	0.5	0.5	0.5	0.4
Forestry (Lumber)	0.8	0.5	0.5	0.6	0.8	1.4	1.5
A SECTOR TOTALS*	**47.8**	**48.6**	**48.6**	**35.7**	**42.7**	**33.3**	**33.5**
M SECTOR:							
Mining	1.4	1.5	1.4	1.8	2.1	2.5	2.6
Factory industry	2.3	2.7	2.8	3.9	5.2	7.9	7.6
Small workshops	9.6	8.6	7.5	9.0	7.1	4.4	4.7
Construction	3.7	3.4	3.8	5.4	3.5	5.7	5.4
M SECTOR TOTALS	**17.0**	**16.2**	**15.5**	**20.1**	**17.9**	**20.5**	**20.3**
S SECTOR:							
Modern transport and communications	3.4	3.4	3.6	4.9	4.6	6.9	7.6
Traditional transport	0.8	0.8	0.8	1.1	1.0	1.0	1.0
Trade	15.4	15.4	15.9	21.2	18.3	17.2	15.9
Government and other services	10.0	10.0	10.0	11.3	9.8	15.3	16.0
Residential rent	5.7	5.7	5.7	5.7	5.7	5.7	5.7
S SECTOR TOTALS	**35.3**	**35.3**	**36.0**	**44.2**	**39.4**	**46.1**	**46.2**

* The sum of the sector totals may differ slightly from 100.0 due to rounding error.

Sources: The same as for table 7 in the *Journal of Economic History* article (see p. 16 above).

Table A-3

PER CAPITA GDP

[Final estimates for table 6, p. 15]

Year	Population	GDP (in million 1934 yuan)	Per capita GDP (yuan)
1924	31,030,000	2,392.6	77.1
1926	32,477,000	2,688.1	82.8
1929	35,759,000	3,049.9	85.3
1934	38,668,000	2,660.0	68.8
1936	39,984,000	3,263.1	81.6
1939	43,035,000	4,149.1	96.4
1941	45,755,000	4,731.1	103.4

Sources: Figures have been revised from table 6 on the basis of the final estimates presented in table A-1.

Table A-4

AVERAGE RATES OF GROWTH

[Final estimates for table 5, p. 14]

(in percent)

	1924-29	1930-35	1936-41	1941
Whole region	5.4	—	7.6	4.1
A sector*	5.3	—	2.4	1.9
M sector	3.0	—	10.4	5.2
S sector	5.4	—	11.1	5.7

* See tables A-1 and A-2 for a list of categories within the A, M, and S sectors.

B. EMPLOYMENT

Beginning in 1934, the Manchurian government compiled labor and employment statistics as part of the police survey and registration of the population. Except for the two cases noted below (salt production and household services), the format and occupational classifications were those used by the Japanese for Japan Proper and for the KTLT in the 1925 and 1930 censuses. The employment data that we have been able to obtain, however, are incomplete and defective in many ways. To illustrate these problems, let us analyze two conflicting sets of data for 1935 (1935-I and 1935-II) and then compare them with data for 1939:[1]

Population by Occupation Group
(in thousands)

	1935-I	1935-II	1939
Agriculture, husbandry, and forestry	9,390	21,755	15,058
Fishing	20	52	41
Mining	123	54	280
Industry	911	952	1,066
Trade	1,093	1,469	1,360
Transport and communications	347	114	132
Government employees and professionals	388	1,154	860
Household services	—	2,743	488
Other occupations	399	1,753	846
TOTAL	**12,671**	**30,046**	**20,131**

General Defects of the Data

Both sets of 1935 data are included under "Population by Occupation Group," yet careful examination shows that this heading really means two different things. The set 1935-I refers to the number of persons actually engaged in the specified occupation, or what is generally known as "employment data." In this set, dependents of employed persons are classified as "people without occupation." The set 1935-II, on the other hand, includes dependents of employed persons, or what should more properly be termed

---

[1] [65], 1939, p. 317; [62], 1938, p. 10; and [37], 1939, p. 9.

"population distribution according to the occupations of family heads." That is why the total for set II is more than double that of set I. If we subtract the total for set II from the population figures in table A-3, we see that there is only a small residual, which represents the people who were truly unemployed and their dependents.

Geographical Coverage. After careful scrutiny, we discovered that set I included the SMR Zone, whereas set II did not. Although the population of the SMR Zone in 1935 was only about half a million, the exclusion of it in set II created tremendous discrepancies in some occupation groups. Since the bulk of the activity in mining and modern transport in Manchuria took place in the SMR Zone, its exclusion made the numbers of people in these two categories in set II smaller than those in set I. Omitting the SMR Zone, on the other hand, had virtually no effect on the data for agriculture and fishing. For those two sectors we can derive the true dependency ratio by comparing the two sets of data. After 1937, the sovereignty of the SMR Zone was returned by Japan to Manchuria, and so data after that year include the SMR Zone. In addition to the omission of the SMR Zone in the figures for set II, all of the employment data exclude the KTLT.

Understatement. As noted above, all of the data exclude the KTLT. Moreover, the general population registrations suffer from understatement. Since the occupation registrations or surveys were undertaken along with the general population registrations, they must embody the same understatement.

Defects of Specific Categories

Agriculture. There is always a serious difficulty in determining "employed persons" in agriculture where the production units are individual families. Although we were unable to obtain the original instructions issued to field workers by the Manchukuo authorities, the resulting statistics clearly show that this problem had not been resolved. The data for 1935-I and 1939 are territorially comparable and both exclude dependents; yet, looking at the numbers of men and women engaged in agriculture, husbandry, and forestry, we find the following increases for the four-year period:[2]

Workers in Agriculture, Husbandry, and Forestry
(in thousands)

	1935-I	1939	Rate of Change
Males	8,624	11,517	33.5%
Females	776	3,541	356.3%
TOTAL	**9,390**	**15,058**	
Females as a ratio of total:	8.1%	23.5%	

---

[2] [65], 1939, p. 317, and [37], 1939, p. 9.

The number of males rose by 33.5%. Further subdivision of males by ethnic group shows that the number of male Koreans and Japanese in this sector rose from 254,000 in 1935 to 351,000 in 1939, or by 38.2%.[3] In view of the Japanese resettlement programs during that period, this increment seems reasonable. Considering the relatively constant figures for farm output in these years, a similar increase in male Chinese (Manchurians) by 2,788,000, or 33.5%, can hardly be accepted as real. Moreover, the dramatic increase in the number of females must be viewed with equal skepticism. The 1935-I figure of 8.1% is far too low to represent the participation of women in agriculture; even 23.5% in 1939 may not be high enough, though it is more believable. Presumably, the increased figures reflect, in part, the improved coverage of the surveys and registrations in the rural areas and, in part, a gradually liberalized definition of "persons employed in agriculture."

Transport and Communications. There was obviously a major definitional change for this occupation group, the result of which was a drastic reduction in the number of persons included in 1939. Although no official explanation has been found, an examination of relevant data suggests that this was a result of eliminating native means of transport, such as carts and carriages operated by farmers either on a part-time basis or during their idle season. The Japanese standard occupational classifications did include these means of transportation,[4] but a Japanese ordinance evidently made some changes in the treatment of those who claimed more than one occupation.[5] This reclassification may also help to explain the increase in male farmers noted above. The ethnic breakdown for this category is as follows:

Workers in Transportation and Communications
(in thousands)

	1935	1939
Chinese	309	95
Non-Chinese	38	37

The large reduction in the Chinese group in this category could account for some of the increase noted in the agricultural figures above.

In 1931, a total of 150,931 people were employed by the railroads in Manchukuo;[6] other transportation systems, such as the highway network, waterway shipping, and harbor facilities, and the communications system had a combined employment of slightly more than 50,000 people. The sum of these is about equal to the sum of the police registration of employment in

---

[3] Ibid.
[4] See [20], p. 100.
[5] Ibid., p. 105.
[6] [50], 1:553.

transportation and communications in Manchuria in 1939, plus the 62,000 people reported for the KTLT in the same category.[7] These figures support the notion that only modern transportation and communications remained in this category.

Salt Production and Household Services. The occupational classifications used by the Manchukuo authorities differed from those in the Japanese census only in these two cases. First, salt production was part of "mining" in the Manchurian classifications but was included under "industry" according to the Japanese classification. This presents no problem for our study since the change is consistent throughout the period. Secondly, the item "household services" was omitted in the Manchurian employment statistics up to 1937. The data for the earlier years, therefore, are not completely comparable with later data.

Armed Forces. The figures for the armed forces were intentionally omitted from the category "government employees and professionals."[8] At the same time, the number of people engaged in "other occupations" rose rapidly during this period, for which there is no satisfactory explanation. There were eight subclassifications under this heading,[9] but the only one that could have expanded by half a million people in just a few years was the catchall category "others." This is most likely the place where the armed forces were concealed.

Methods of Handling the Defects

The general shortcomings mentioned above are not too harmful. For our purposes, we simply selected the set of employment data which included the SMR Zone but excluded dependents, i.e., 1935-I. Although these employment data reflect the same downward bias as the police registrations of the population, the percentage distribution of the data should nonetheless be meaningful and usable. That is to say, if the official count of the total population in a given year falls short of the true size by 5%, then the percentage distribution is just a result based on a sample of 95% of the population. This result should not be rejected unless there are systematic biases; for example, if the 5% of the population not covered by the sample was actually concentrated in one or two sectors. We have no reason to suspect systematic bias. Based on the above reasoning, we use the percentage distribution of population among various occupations, together with our estimates of total population, to derive a new set of employment data. Finally, we add the employment data of the KTLT, which are readily available, to obtain the figures for all of Manchuria.

---

[7] [67], 1943, p. 4.

[8] There was a subset "servicemen in armed forces" in this category, but the entry was left blank in each report. The figures of the remaining subclassifications add up to exactly the subtotal. See [37], 1939, p. 9, and 1942, p. 8.

[9] [20], p. 101.

Particularly troublesome are the specific shortcomings involving either definitional changes or shifts between occupational groups. In some cases, virtually no adjustment can be made without access to detailed statistics. Fortunately, we have output statistics for the groups with definitional changes: agriculture and transport and communications. Since we need employment data primarily for the purpose of computing national income originating in various sectors, we can compute value-added figures directly from the output statistics for these cases and omit them from our employment data tabulation.

The omission of "household services" in the employment data for the early years does not create a serious problem. Employment in this category was fairly stable in both China Proper and Manchuria in the prewar period. Thus, on the basis of data for later years, it is not unreasonable to assume a constant ratio of household services to total population.

The category "other occupations" is merged with "government employees and professionals" on the following grounds: first, the subclasses of "other occupations" were on the government payrolls, even though the employees were not white-collar workers; and second, the residual subclass "others" must have included the armed forces and/or other people engaged in low-income jobs. To handle all of them in the same fashion as the armed forces would not create a sizable margin of error in our estimates of national income. The results of our computations and adjustments for the selected occupation groups are presented in tables B-1 and B-2.

Table B–1

DISTRIBUTION OF WORKERS IN SELECTED
OCCUPATIONS IN MANCHURIA (EXCLUDING KTLT), 1934-41
(expressed as percentages of total population)

	1934	1936	1939	1941
Fishing	0.06	0.06	0.10	0.10
Mining	0.34	0.35	0.71	0.69
Industry	2.62	2.59	2.71	2.97
Trade	3.04	3.09	3.46	3.42
Household services	1.00	1.00	1.25	1.02
Government employees, professionals, and others	2.18	2.20	4.39	4.88

Sources: 1934: [41], 1937, p. 8. 1936: [41], 1939, p. 17. 1939: [67], no. 3 (1943), p. 4. 1941: [37], 1942, p. 6. "Household services" was omitted in the official statistics for 1934 and 1936. It is assumed to be 1% of total population in both years.

Table B-2

WORKERS IN SELECTED OCCUPATIONS
IN MANCHURIA AND THE KTLT, 1934-41
(in thousands)

	1934	*1936*	*1939*	*1941*
Fishing				
Manchuria	23	23	42	44
KTLT	16	17	19	21
TOTAL	**39**	**40**	**61**	**65**
Mining				
Manchuria	128	136	297	305
KTLT	2	3	6	9
TOTAL	**130**	**139**	**303**	**314**
Industry				
Manchuria	986	1,006	1,132	1,315
KTLT	55	73	91	110
TOTAL	**1,041**	**1,079**	**1,223**	**1,425**
Trade				
Manchuria	1,144	1,200	1,445	1,514
KTLT	63	79	79	83
TOTAL	**1,207**	**1,279**	**1,524**	**1,597**
Household services				
Manchuria	376	388	522	451
KTLT	12	11	45	50
TOTAL	**388**	**399**	**567**	**501**
Government employees, professionals, and others				
Manchuria	821	854	1,834	2,160
KTLT	60	68	52	62
TOTAL	**881**	**922**	**1,886**	**2,222**

Sources: All of the figures for Manchuria were derived from the percentages given in table B-1 and the population figures given in table A-3. The KTLT figures are from [25], pp. 74-101, and [67], no. 3 (1963), p. 4.

C. AGRICULTURE

The agricultural sector is here defined as consisting of two types of production: (a) crops and (b) livestock and related products. Our procedure for estimating value–added figures in this sector was to collect physical output data for all components of agricultural output and their 1934 prices in order to compute the gross value of agricultural production. Deductible costs were then estimated and subtracted so as to arrive at the value–added figures in table C-16. The many data gaps encountered in the actual computations had to be bridged by imputed figures and proxies.

Tables C-1 through C-6 show the derivation of gross values for crop production, and tables C-7 through C-14 indicate the gross values for livestock and related products. Table C-15 summarizes the ratios of deductible costs. It should be noted that since the prices used here to compute gross values were wholesale prices in major cities, they include the cost of transporting farm products from the countryside to the cities. Such transport was performed almost exclusively by traditional means, i.e., carts. We could either deduct such costs here or exclude such activities in the computations for traditional transport (section L). The latter approach was taken because it simplifies our whole computation. The final results for the value–added of agriculture in various years are presented in table C-16.

Table C-1

GRAIN PRODUCTION

(in thousand metric tons)

	1924	1925	1926	1927	1928	1929	1930
Soybeans	3,448	4,173	4,776	4,817	4,834	4,849	5,298
Kaoliang	4,453	4,682	4,526	4,580	4,613	4,681	4,780
Millet	3,027	3,121	2,967	3,209	3,274	3,352	3,276
Corn	1,620	1,810	1,704	1,714	1,742	1,613	1,586
Wheat	805	961	968	1,445	1,470	1,302	1,357
Paddy rice	94	192	180	148	150	137	154
Upland rice	88	150	133	147	144	156	158
Other beans	244	352	415	435	471	377	370
Other grains	754	885	822	1,012	1,254	1,594	1,723

	1931	1932	1933	1934	1935	1936	1937
Soybeans	5,227	4,268	4,601	3,398	3,859	4,147	4,352
Kaoliang	4,497	3,729	4,022	3,469	4,103	4,241	4,315
Millet	2,960	2,615	3,184	2,123	2,968	3,187	3,226
Corn	1,701	1,542	1,759	1,502	1,903	2,072	2,240
Wheat	1,580	1,133	863	643	1,015	959	1,126
Paddy rice	159	110	166	200	296	442	549
Upland rice	163	137	143	126	147	155	140
Other beans	313	278	304	277	326	341	327
Other grains	1,853	1,550	1,804	1,046	1,106	1,093	1,069

	1938	1939	1940	1941	1942
Soybeans	4,612	3,819	3,371	3,381	3,025
Kaoliang	4,680	4,464	4,775	4,878	4,755
Millet	3,134	3,065	3,588	3,620	3,332
Corn	2,400	2,332	2,778	3,133	3,189
Wheat	976	889	762	884	692
Paddy rice	619	743	610	724	532
Upland rice	131	102	99	84	49
Other beans	362	307	405	407	339
Other grains	1,114	1,017	1,182	1,439	1,513

Sources: 1924-32: [97], p. 260, except for "other beans," 1924 and 1925: [50], 1:813. 1933-42: [82], pp. 282-83.

Table C-2

AGRICULTURAL PRICES, 1934

	Original quotation	Price per metric ton (in yuan)
Soybeans	3.46 yuan per 100 chin	57.7
Kaoliang	2.55 yuan per 100 chin	42.5
Millet	3.80 yuan per 100 chin	63.3
Corn	2.41 yuan per 100 chin	40.2
Wheat	1.17 yuan per 27.25 chin	114.1
Paddy rice		87.1
Upland rice		96.3
Other beans		42.8
Other grains		74.1

Sources: With the exceptions noted below, prices are 1934 Fengtien wholesale prices obtained from [9], 1936. The 1934 prices for "other beans" and "other grains" are imputed from the 1934 soybean price and the price ratio between soybeans and other beans and grains in 1930 as given in [72]. The prices for rice are imputed from the Dairen price ratio between rice and soybeans in 1934. [72] indicates that the price of upland rice was about 10% higher than that of paddy rice. So we raise the price of paddy rice by 10% and use the resulting figures as the imputed price of upland rice.

Table C-3

GROSS VALUES OF GRAIN CROPS
(in million 1934 yuan)

	1924	1926	1929	1934	1936	1939	1941
Soybeans	198.9	275.6	279.8	196.1	239.3	220.3	195.1
Kaoliang	189.2	192.3	198.9	147.4	180.2	189.7	207.3
Millet	191.6	187.8	212.2	134.4	201.7	194.0	229.1
Corn	65.1	68.5	64.8	60.4	83.3	93.7	125.9
Wheat	91.8	110.4	148.6	73.4	109.4	101.4	100.9
Paddy rice	8.2	15.7	11.9	17.4	38.5	64.7	63.1
Upland rice	8.5	12.8	15.0	12.1	14.9	9.8	8.1
Other beans	10.4	17.8	16.1	11.9	14.6	13.1	17.4
Other grains	55.9	60.9	118.1	77.5	81.0	75.4	106.6
TOTAL	**819.6**	**941.8**	**1,065.4**	**730.6**	**962.9**	**962.1**	**1,053.5**

Sources: Computed from the output data in table C-1 and prices in table C-2.

Table C-4

OUTPUT OF FRUITS AND VEGETABLES

| | FRUITS | | | VEGETABLES |
| | KTLT and SMR Zone | | Whole Manchuria | |
Year	Gross value (in thousand current yuan) (1)	Price index (1934 = 100) (2)	Gross value (in thousand 1934 yuan) (3)	Gross value (in thousand 1934 yuan) (4)	Gross value (in thousand 1934 yuan) (5)
1924	366	172.0	213	284	65,568
1926	542	146.2	371	495	75,344
1929	834	138.5	602	803	85,232
1934	1,882	100.0	1,882	2,509	58,448
1936	1,624	143.6	1,131	1,508	77,032
1939	2,603	245.9	1,059	1,412	76,968
1941	6,232	285.0	2,187	2,916	84,820

Sources: Col. (1): 1924-34: [25], table 53, pp. 276-78; 1936-41: [26], no. 36 (1941), pp. 70-71. Col. (2): These are Dairen price indexes; see [68], various years. Col. (3): Col. (1) deflated by the price indexes in col. (2). Col. (4): According to [75], p. 28, about two-thirds of the total fruit acreage was in the KTLT and SMR Zone. Assuming that the unit yield was lower in the rest of Manchuria and that the remaining one-third of fruit acreage produced only one-quarter of the total fruit output in whole Manchuria, we derive col. (4) from col. (3). Col. (5): There is no way to estimate vegetable output directly for whole Manchuria. According to [34], table E-1, the gross value of vegetables was about 6% of the total gross value of grain crops in China in 1933. On the other hand, statistics of the KTLT show that the ratio revolved around 12% up to 1936-37 (see [25], pp. 276-78, and [26], p. 71). We take 8% as the ratio for whole Manchuria. Using this ratio and the total gross values of grain crops as given in table C-3, we derive the gross output values of vegetables for various years.

Table C-5
OUTPUT OF INDUSTRIAL CROPS*

Year	Industrial crop acreage (as % of grain crops) (1)	Value adjustment factor (2)	Gross value of grain crops (in million 1934 yuan) (3)	Gross value of industrial crops (in million 1934 yuan) (4)
1924	2.3	1.00	819.6	18.8
1926	2.3	1.00	941.8	21.7
1929	2.3	1.00	1,065.4	24.5
1934	6.0	1.30	730.6	57.0
1936	6.7	1.18	962.9	76.1
1939	7.8	1.17	962.1	87.8
1941	8.0	1.83	1,053.5	154.2

* "Industrial crops" includes cotton, tobacco, peanuts, sesame oil, oil seeds, and flax.

Sources: Col. (1): 1924-26: 1929 ratio is used; 1929: [34], 1929, p. 25; 1934-41: [82], 1943, pp. 280-81. Col. (2): The per acre yield in value terms may not be the same for grains and industrial crops. Unfortunately, no information on the presence or extent of this variation could be obtained for all of Manchuria. The only indication is given in the KTLT data, which we utilize to compute the average value of industrial crops per acre as a ratio of the average value of grain crops per acre. We call this the "value adjustment factor." The relevant information is found in [25], tables 51 and 53, and [26], no. 37 (1942), pp. 62-70. The results are shown in the table below. Col. (3): Table C-3. Col. (4): Col. (1) x col. (3).

Year	Industrial crop acreage (as % of grain crop average in KTLT)	Value of industrial crops (as % of value of grain crops in KTLT)	Value adjustment factor
1929	1.0	1.0	1.00
1934	1.0	1.3	1.30
1936	1.1	1.3	1.18
1939	1.2	1.4	1.17
1941	1.2	2.2	1.83

Table C-6

GROSS VALUE OF ALL CROPS

(in million 1934 yuan)

	1924	1926	1929	1934	1936	1939	1941
Grains	819.6	941.8	1,065.4	730.6	962.9	962.1	1,053.5
Fruits	0.3	0.5	0.8	2.5	1.5	1.4	2.9
Vegetables	65.6	75.3	85.2	58.5	77.0	77.0	84.3
Industrial crops	18.8	21.7	24.5	57.0	76.1	87.8	154.2
Miscellaneous crops	45.2	52.0	58.8	42.4	55.9	56.4	64.7
TOTAL	**949.5**	**1,091.3**	**1,234.7**	**891.0**	**1,173.4**	**1,184.7**	**1,359.6**

Sources: Tables C-3, C-4, and C-5. The value of "miscellaneous crops" is assumed to be 5% of the total in each year.

Table C-7

LIVESTOCK

(in thousand head)

	1924	1926	1928	1929	1933	1934	1935
Cattle	2,000	—	1,527	1,605	1,500	1,164	1,277
Horses	2,500	2,410	2,426	2,422	1,967	1,623	1,807
Mules	620	552	656	739	750	612	568
Donkeys	600	566	468	467	375	570	621
Sheep and goats	2,000	—	2,549	2,602	1,929	1,421	2,058
Pigs	—	—	7,537	7,352	5,304	4,964	6,099
Chickens	—	—	—	12,034	—	8,480	8,480
Geese and ducks	—	—	—	2,678	—	1,380	1,380

	1936	1937	1938	1939	1940	1941
Cattle	1,421	1,633	1,768	1,820	1,873	1,900
Horses	1,809	1,824	1,838	1,755	1,825	1,899
Mules	621	617	613	609	605	601
Donkeys	568	564	560	555	550	546
Sheep and goats	2,432	3,210	3,823	3,754	3,476	3,473
Pigs	5,911	5,336	5,107	4,702	4,597	4,213
Chickens	8,480	—	7,863	7,327	7,938	6,636
Geese and ducks	1,380	—	1,256	1,352	1,406	1,218

Sources: 1924: [61], 1928, pp. 524-26. 1926: J. B. Condliffe, *Problems of the Pacific, 1929* (Chicago, 1930), p. 390. 1928: [84], 1929, p. 18. 1929-34: [50], 1:821. For poultry, the 1930 figures in [72] are used for 1929, and the 1935 figures are used for 1934. 1935: [51], 1938, p. 799. 1936: For horses, mules, and donkeys, data are from [53], p. 252. For poultry, the 1935 figures are used. For other animals, see [51], 1938, p. 799. 1937-41: For cattle, sheep and goats, pigs, chickens, and geese and ducks, data are from [67], no. 3 (1943), pp. 26-27. For mules and donkeys, data for 1943 are from the U.S. government publication *Stock Breeding in Northeast China*, p. 9: mules = 590; donkeys = 538,000. We simply interpolate for the interim years. For horses, data are from [35], pp. 335-40, and from [41], 1939, p. 518.

Table C-8

CHANGES IN LIVESTOCK VALUE

(values in thousand 1934 yuan)

		1928-29	1933-34	1935-36	1938-39	1940-41
Cattle	(#)	+77,750	-366,160	+144,494	+51,111	+27,016
	(value)	+7,184	-31,061	+13,351	+4,723	+2,496
Horses	(#)	-3,540	-344,385	+2,000	-83,000	+74,000
	(value)	-569	-55,377	+322	-13,346	+11,899
Mules	(#)	+8,314	-138,362	+53,000	-4,000	-4,000
	(value)	+16,561	-27,562	+10,558	-797	-797
Donkeys	(#)	-1,090	+195,160	-53,000	-5,000	-4,000
	(value)	-33	+5,855	-1,590	-150	-120
Sheep and	(#)	+52,570	-508,159	+374,482	-68,946	-3,340
goats	(value)	+694	-6,708	+4,943	-910	-44
Pigs	(#)	-185,170	-339,375	-187,336	-405,195	-383,797
	(value)	-6,000	-10,996	-6,070	-13,128	-12,435
TOTAL		**+17,837**	**-125,849**	**+21,514**	**-23,608**	**+999**

Sources: The raw quantities are from table C-7. We use rounded figures in that table because the numbers are too large for tabulation. Here the annual increments are in unrounded figures. Values are computed with the following prices per head (in yuan): cattle, 92.4; horses, 160.8; mules, 199.2; donkeys, 30.0; sheep and goats, 13.2; pigs, 32.4. The prices were originally the 1930 prices from [72], but they have been converted into 1934 prices by using the price indexes of meat between the years 1930-34. See [68], 1935-36, p. 56.

Table C-9

MEAT PRODUCTION

(meat in metric tons,

values in thousand 1934 yuan)

		1929	1934	1936	1939	1941
Cattle	(#)*	157,000	133,000	135,000	179,000	189,000
	(meat)	17,229	14,648	14,839	19,739	20,756
	(value)	8,316	7,701	7,163	9,528	10,019
Sheep and	(#)	901,000	586,000	786,000	1,326,000	1,216,000
goats	(meat)	12,619	8,206	11,000	18,564	17,025
	(value)	8,041	5,229	7,009	11,829	10,848
Pigs	(#)	5,955,000	4,107,000	4,804,000	3,924,000	3,524,000
	(meat)	297,761	205,364	240,193	196,182	176,184
	(value)	205,783	141,927	165,997	135,581	121,761
Chickens	(#)	12,034,000	8,480,000	8,480,000	7,595,000	7,287,000
	(meat)	9,025	6,300	6,300	5,696	5,465
	(value)	5,401	3,771	3,771	3,409	3,271
Ducks and	(#)	2,678,000	1,380,000	1,380,000	1,304,000	1,312,000
geese	(meat)	2,008	1,035	1,035	978	984
	(value)	947	483	483	457	459
TOTAL VALUE		**228,478**	**158,481**	**184,423**	**160,804**	**146,358**

* Represents the number of animals slaughtered.

Sources: For the number of animals slaughtered, we use two-year averages of the numbers of livestock (as derived from table C-7) and multiply those figures by their respective slaughter rates. The slaughter rates, from [12], p. 214, and [43], 1940, p. 567, are as follows: cattle, 10%; sheep and goats, 35%; pigs, 80%; chickens, 100%; ducks and geese, 100%. For the amount of meat produced, we multiply the number of slaughtered animals by the figures for meat per head. The figures for meat per head, also from [12], p. 214, and [43], 1940, p. 567, are as follows: cattle, 110 kg; sheep and goats, 14 kg; pigs, 50 kg; chickens, 0.75 kg; ducks and geese, 0.75 kg. For the meat production values, we multiply the amount of meat produced by the price. Dairen 1934 wholesale prices for beef, pork, and chicken meat are given in [24], 1941, p. 2. For mutton, we apply the beef to mutton retail price ratio (as revealed in [9], 1939, p. 41) to our wholesale beef price. The price for duck and goose meat was 78% of the price for chicken. See Alexander Eckstein, *The National Income of Communist China* (New York, 1962), p. 95. The prices used to determine the value of meat production are as follows (in yuan per metric ton): cattle, 482.7; sheep and goats, 637.2; pigs, 691.1; chickens, 598.5; ducks and goose, 466.8.

Table C-10

EGG PRODUCTION

(numbers in millions,
values in million 1934 yuan)

		1929	1934	1936	1939	1941
Chicken	(#)	541.5	381.6	381.6	329.7	298.6
	(value)	17.2	12.1	12.1	10.4	9.5
Duck	(#)	93.7	48.3	48.3	47.3	42.6
	(value)	3.9	2.0	2.0	2.0	1.8
TOTAL VALUE		**21.1**	**14.1**	**14.1**	**12.4**	**11.3**

Sources: Derived from table C-7. It is assumed that 50% of the poultry were female and thus egg-laying. The rates of eggs laid per head per year are 90 for chicken and 70 for ducks and geese. See [12], p. 213. The 1934 wholesale prices per 100 eggs were 3.17 yuan for chicken and 4.22 yuan for ducks and geese. See [68], 1934, and [34], p. 355.

Table C-11

ANIMAL HIDE PRODUCTION

(numbers in thousands,
values in thousand 1934 yuan)

		1928-29	1933-34	1935-36	1938-39	1940-41
Cattle	(#)	157	133	135	179	189
	(value)	3,007	2,557	2,590	3,445	3,622
Horses	(#)	121	90	90	90	93
	(value)	582	431	431	431	447
Mules	(#)	35	34	30	31	30
	(value)	167	163	144	147	145
Donkeys	(#)	23	24	30	28	27
	(value)	112	113	144	134	130
Sheep and	(#)	901	586	786	1,326	1,216
goats	(value)	2,975	1,934	2,593	4,376	4,013
Dogs, cats, and						
rabbits	(#)	991	452	517	768	756
	(value)	594	452	517	768	756
TOTAL VALUE		**7,437**	**5,651**	**6,420**	**9,302**	**9,113**

Sources: The slaughter rates (from [12], p. 214) are as follows: cattle, 10%; horses, 5%; mules, 5%; donkeys, 5%; sheep and goats, 35%. Because the livestock numbers as stated in the sources refer to year-end figures, we use two-year averages of livestock numbers (see table C-7) and apply the slaughter rates to them to get the numbers of hides and skins. The number of dogs, cats, and rabbits slaughtered in 1929 is given in [84], 1931, p. 31. The 1930 prices are taken from [72], pp. 25-26, and are then adjusted according to the meat price index betweeen 1930 and 1934 (see [68], 1935-36, p. 56). The value of skins of dogs, cats, and rabbits in 1929 was about 6% of the total value of hide and skin production in that year. We use the same percentage for the other years listed. The 1934 prices for animal skins are as follows (in yuan per sheet): cattle, 192; horses, 48; mules, 48; donkeys, 48; sheep and goats, 33; dogs, cats, and rabbits, 6.

Table C-12

WOOL PRODUCTION

	1929	1934	1936	1939	1941
Quantity (in metric tons)	2,009	1,306	1,751	2,955	2,711
Value (in thousand 1934 yuan)	1,338	870	1,166	1,968	1,806

Sources: Since the livestock numbers in the sources refer to year-end figures, we take the two-year average of numbers of sheep and goats (table C-7) and assume that 65% of them were sheared in any given year (see [56], p. 209) and that 1.2 kg of wool was obtained per head (see [56], p. 11). The price of wool was 666 yuan per metric ton (see [60], p. 51).

Table C-13

HOG BRISTLE PRODUCTION

	1929	1934	1936	1939	1941
Quantity (in metric tons)	1,787	1,232	1,441	1,177	1,057
Value (in thousand 1934 yuan)	7,445	5,132	6,003	4,903	4,403

Sources: According to [56], p. 11, 0.3 kg. of bristle could be obtained per head of hog, and the average price is quoted as 4,166 yuan per metric ton. Again, two-year averages are used to determine the number of hogs in the years listed above, and the slaughter rate, given in the sources for table C-9, is 80%.

Table C-14

GROSS VALUE OF LIVESTOCK AND PRODUCTS
(in million 1934 yuan)

	1929	1934	1936	1939	1941
Increment in livestock (in thousand head)	+14.8	-125.8	+21.5	-23.6	+1.0
Meat production	228.5	158.5	184.4	160.8	146.0
Egg production	21.1	14.1	14.1	12.4	11.3
Animal hide production	7.4	5.7	6.4	9.3	9.1
Wool production	1.3	0.9	1.2	2.0	1.8
Hog bristle production	7.4	5.1	6.0	4.9	4.4
Miscellaneous	14.0	2.9	11.7	8.3	8.7
TOTAL	**294.5**	**61.4**	**245.3**	**174.1**	**182.3**

Sources: Tables C-8, C-9, C-10, C-11, C-12, and C-13. "Miscellaneous" is assumed to be 5% of the total.

Table C-15

ESTIMATES OF AGRICULTURAL INPUTS

		% of gross value
Crops		
Seeds	(1)	4.80
Fertilizer	(2)	3.20
Repair and maintenance of buildings	(3)	0.27
Repair and maintenance of implements	(4)	0.28
TOTAL	(5)	8.55
Livestock		
Feed	(6)	21.50

Sources: Row (1): [72]. Row (2): [87], pp. 9-15. Row (3): [64], table 4. Row (4): [64], table 5. Row (5): Sum of rows 1-4. Row (6): [72].

Table C-16

VALUE-ADDED OF AGRICULTURE

(in million 1934 yuan)

		1924	1926	1929	1934	1936	1939	1941
Gross Value								
Crops	(1)	949.5	1,091.3	1,234.7	891.0	1,173.4	1,184.7	1,359.6
Livestock and products	(2)	229.8	264.1	297.7	61.4	245.3	174.1	182.3
Total	(3)	1,179.3	1,355.4	1,532.4	952.4	1,418.7	1,358.8	1,541.9
Inputs								
Crops	(4)	81.2	93.3	105.6	76.2	100.3	101.3	116.3
Livestock and products	(5)	49.4	56.8	64.0	13.2	52.7	37.4	39.2
Total	(6)	130.6	150.1	169.6	89.4	153.0	138.7	155.5
TOTAL VALUE-ADDED	**(7)**	**1,048.7**	**1,205.3**	**1,362.8**	**863.0**	**1,265.7**	**1,220.1**	**1,386.4**

Sources: Row (1): Table C-6. Row (2): Table C-14. In 1929, "livestock and products" was about 24.2% of the total crop value. The same percentage is applied to 1924 and 1926. Row (3): Row (1) + row (2). Row (4): 8.55% x row (1) (see table C-15). Row (5): 21.5% x row (2) (see table C-15). Row (6): Row (4) + row (5). Row (7): Row (3) - row (6).

D. SUBSIDIARY PRODUCTION OF FARMERS

In addition to farming the land and raising livestock and poultry, Chinese farmers generally engaged in a wide variety of subsidiary production activities during the idle season. Since our estimates of agricultural production are based on crop and livestock product values, value-added by farmers in subsidiary lines of production is not included. It is also missing in the estimates for industry and fishing because the producers were not industrial workers or fishermen by occupation.

In 1936, the Manchukuo government conducted a survey of the subsidiary production of farmers in all of Manchuria, the results of which were published the following year. The survey listed the following subsidiary production lines:

(1) thirteen activities related to agricultural products, e.g., mat weaving, brewing, flour milling, noodle making, bean curd production, vegetable pickling;

(2) ten activities related to forest products, including charcoal production, the collection and processing of medicinal herbs, furniture production;

(3) eight activites related to animal husbandry, e.g., making blankets and fur clothing;

(4) four activities related to marine products, e.g., the salting of fish;

(5) four activities in the category "others," e.g., the production of ceramics.

According to the survey, gross earnings from these subsidiary production activities totaled 137.4 million yuan in 1936 prices,[1] or about 7.6% of the value-added of agriculture proper when measured in current yuan in that year.[2] Since these activities were only sidelines for farmers, operational costs were kept to a minimum. We assume that 10% of the gross earnings covered the operational

---

[1] See [38], p. 3.

[2] The value-added of agriculture proper in 1936 was about 1,266 million yuan in 1934 constant prices (see table C-16). The Dairen price index of grains between 1934 and 1936 was 143.6 (see [68], 1940, p. 56). Thus, the total value-added at current prices in 1936, including value-added of subsidiary production of farmers, would be 1,818 million yuan.

costs. Thus, the income from these lines of production, including depreciation, would be 6.8% of the value-added in agriculture proper. In the absence of comparable data for other years, we use the same ratio for all years to estimate the value-added of subsidiary production of farmers. The results, stated in millions of 1934 yuan, are given in table D.

Table D

VALUE-ADDED OF SUBSIDIARY PRODUCTION OF FARMERS

(in million 1934 yuan)

Year	Value-added
1924	72.2
1926	83.0
1929	92.7
1934	58.7
1936	86.1
1939	83.0
1941	94.3

E. FISHING

The estimation of value-added of the fishing sector is straightforward. There is one output series, as measured by annual catches, and it is divided into three separate geographical systems: (1) fishing along the coast of the KTLT; (2) fishing along the Manchurian coasts of the Yellow Sea and the Po Sea; and (3) fishing in inland waters. We have compiled the reported catches in quantitative terms for each of the three areas and computed the output index for the selected benchmark years (see table E-1). It should be pointed out that these statistics cover both the output of modern fishing establishments and the output of individual fishermen using traditional methods and equipment.

The official estimate of net value-added of Manchurian fishing, excluding the KTLT, was 38.8 million yuan for 1941. This amount may be enlarged to represent the net value-added of fishing in the whole of Manchuria by using the ratio of catches in the KTLT to catches in all of Manchuria (see table E-1). The resulting figure is 62.2 million yuan. This amount is, however, net of depreciation, which has been estimated at 2% of net value-added in China.[1] We employ the same rate to convert net value-added into gross value-added, then apply the output indexes to our gross value-added figures to obtain the value-added amounts for other years. This set of value figures, which is in 1941 prices, is then deflated into 1934 yuan.

It is reported that in 1934, catches of fish in the KTLT totaled 11,716,943 kuan (a Japanese weight unit of which 266.66 = one metric ton), which was valued at 5,016,444 yuan in current prices. Total KTLT catches in 1941 amounted to 14,302,949 kuan, which was worth 22,883,754 yuan in 1941 prices.[2] These data imply a price index of 373.7% for this sector between 1934 and 1941. We use this deflator to convert all values from 1941 yuan to 1934 yuan. The results are presented in table E-1.

---

[1] See [34], pp. 139, 419.
[2] See [50], 1:837.

Table E-1

FISHING CATCHES

(in tons)

		1924	1926	1929	1934	1936	1939	1941
MANCHURIA								
(excluding KTLT)								
Inland waters	(1)	16,000	17,350	19,376	46,425	52,378	—	—
Coastal	(2)	4,280	14,188	23,964	27,311	19,452	—	—
Total	(3)	20,280	31,538	43,340	73,736	71,830	94,901	88,792
KTLT	(4)	10,725	14,580	48,116	43,939	56,839	71,516	53,636
WHOLE								
MANCHURIA								
Index (1934 = 100)	(5)	26.3	39.2	77.7	100.0	109.3	141.4	121.0
TOTAL	**(6)**	**31,005**	**46,118**	**91,456**	**117,675**	**128,669**	**166,417**	**142,428**

Sources: Row (1): 1924: [74], p. 87; 1926: interpolated; 1929: [36], 1933, p. 618; 1934 and 1936: row (3) - row (2). Row (2): 1924: [50], p. 830; 1926: [97], 1931, p. 1378; 1929, 1934, and 1936: [68], 1935-36, p. 147. Row (3): 1924, 1926, and 1929: row (1) + row (2); 1934 and 1936: [65], 1938, p. 1; 1939 and 1941: [67], no. 3 (1943), p. 28. Row (4): All years: [50], p. 837. Row (5): See text. Row (6): Row (3) + row (4).

Table E-2

VALUE-ADDED OF FISHING

	1924	1926	1929	1934	1936	1939	1941
Million 1941 yuan	13.8	20.6	40.7	52.4	57.4	74.2	63.5
Million 1934 yuan	3.7	5.5	11.0	14.1	15.4	20.0	17.1

Sources: See the text for this section.

F. PRODUCTION OF LUMBER

Production indexes are here reckoned on the basis of lumber output in various years. The official estimate of net value-added in 1941 is known to have been 237.2 million yuan in current prices. Although this figure does not include the KTLT, it is representative of Manchuria as a whole because no lumber was produced in the KTLT.

Gross value-added is derived by adding 5% to the above figure.[1] The gross value-added of 1941 is then applied to the output index in order to obtain value-added figures in other years. These values are then converted into 1934 yuan by using the wholesale price index of lumber (344.1%) in Dairen between 1934 and 1941.

---

[1] The depreciation rate is estimated on the basis of the rate for China given in [34], p. 514.

Table F

LUMBER PRODUCTION

Year	Output quantity (in cubic meters) (1)	Output index (1934 = 100) (2)	Value-added (in million 1941 yuan) (3)	Value-added (in million 1934 yuan) (4)
1924	1,353,827	120.7	68.3	19.9
1926	939,393	83.7	47.4	13.8
1929	1,070,227	95.4	54.0	15.7
1934	1,121,849	100.0	56.6	16.4
1936	1,845,493	164.5	93.1	27.1
1939	4,070,419	362.8	205.3	59.6
1941	4,950,264	441.3	249.7	72.6

Sources: Col. (1): 1924-34: data are given in [50], 1:825 (they are originally stated in tan and have been converted into cubic meters at the rate of one tan = 0.2782 cubic meters); 1936 and 1939: [67], no. 3 (1943), p. 32; 1941: [3], p. 14. Col. (2): Computed from col. (1). Col. (3): The 1941 figure is from [3], p. 14, plus 5% depreciation charges. Others are derived by using the index in col. (2). Col. (4): Derived from col. (3) using a deflator of 344.1%, which is taken from [24], 1941, p. 7.

G. MINING

The estimation of value–added in this sector begins with the production quantities for individual mining products in various years. Included here are seven major items which accounted for about 96% of total mining production in Manchuria in 1933.[1] The output figures include the production of indigenous mines using premodern methods. This is confirmed by the 1934 figures for gold output. For instance, gold was generally mined by traditional methods until the establishment of the Manchuria Gold Mining Company in 1934.

Factory prices (i.e., the prices at which the mining companies sold the commodities before the products were transported to markets) have been collected, and the ratios of deductible costs for various products have been determined. One source of cost data for coal and shale oil is a volume of official budget and production costs of the Fushun Coal Mine,[2] which was a producer of these two items. For other mining products, the ratios derived by Ou Pao–san, who made the first national income estimate for China Proper, are adopted here because of the absence of similar data for Manchuria. These ratios enable us to compute the annual value–added in each sector. The whole derivation procedure can be seen in the tables for this section.

---

[1] See [57], 2:57.
[2] See [17].

Table G–1

MINING PRODUCTION

(in thousand metric tons unless otherwise specified)

	1924	1926	1929	1934	1936	1939	1941
Coal	6,959	7,995	10,251	11,828	13,874	19,000	23,800
Iron ore	824	1,117	986	1,133	1,795	3,076	3,703
Gold (in kg)	1,600	1,674	525	464	3,977	3,500	3,900
Limestone	256	270	630	636	602	668	854
Shale oil	—	—	—	91	180	360	600
Magnesite	10	20	32	100	191	593	602
Salt	571	775	528	418	785	1,200	1,229

Sources: Coal: 1924-34: [57], no. 5, pp. 34-35; 1936-41: [58], p. 74. Iron ore: 1924: according to [84], 1933, output of pig iron increased by 35.6% between 1924 and 1926, and this rate of increase is used to extrapolate the output of iron ore between 1924 and 1926; 1926-29: [84], 1933; 1934-36: [88], nos. 5-6, table 9; 1939-41: [67], no. 2 (1943). Gold: 1924-34: [68], various years; 1936: [28], 1940, p. 616; 1939-41: [67], no. 2 (1943). Limestone: 1924-29: [80], pp. 40-42; 1934-36: [28], 1938, p. 595; 1939-41: [67], no. 3 (1943). Shale oil (production began in 1930): 1934: [57], nos. 4-5; 1936-41: [57], no. 7. Magnesite: 1924-29: [80], pp. 40-42; 1934-36: [88], nos. 5-6; 1939-41: [67], no. 3 (1943). Salt: 1924-36: [28], various years; 1939-41: [67], no. 3 (1943).

Table G-2

FACTORY PRICES AND RATIOS OF DEDUCTIBLE COSTS
FOR MINING PRODUCTS, 1934

	Factory prices (in yuan per metric ton)	% of deductible costs in prices
Coal	3.62	35%
Iron ore	7.60	7%
Gold (prices in yuan/kg)	2,598.00	25%
Limestone	2.70	15%
Shale oil	26.80	66%
Magnesite	14.80	25%
Salt	20.00	45%

Sources: Price data for the following items are from [66]: Coal, p. 208; iron ore, p. 115; gold, p. 144; limestone, p. 288; shale oil, p. 200; magnesite, p. 281 (the price of salt is from [48], p. 79). The deductible cost ratios of iron ore, gold, limestone, and magnesite are from [57], 2:52. The ratios for coal and shale oil are computed from the cost information in [17], pp. 3, 49, 53, 54. The ratio for salt is from [48], p. 79.

Table G-3

GROSS VALUES OF MINING PRODUCTION

(in million 1934 yuan)

	1924	1926	1929	1934	1936	1939	1941
Coal	25.19	28.94	37.11	42.82	50.22	68.78	86.16
Iron ore	6.26	8.49	7.49	8.61	13.64	23.38	28.14
Gold	4.16	4.35	1.36	1.20	10.33	9.09	10.13
Limestone	0.69	0.73	1.70	1.71	1.63	1.80	2.31
Shale oil	—	—	—	2.44	4.82	9.65	16.08
Magnesite	0.15	0.29	0.47	1.48	2.83	8.78	8.91
Salt	11.42	15.50	10.56	8.36	15.70	24.00	24.58
Miscellaneous	1.68	2.04	2.05	2.33	3.47	5.09	6.17
TOTAL	**49.55**	**60.34**	**60.74**	**68.95**	**102.64**	**150.57**	**182.48**

Sources: Except for "miscellaneous," the gross values are computed from the physical quantities (table G-1) and the unit prices (table G-2). Only seven major products have been included here. However, [57], no. 5, gives a more complete list of mining outputs in Manchuria in 1933 value terms. According to that calculation, the combined value of the items omitted in our study amounts to 3.5% of the total value of products included here. Using this ratio uniformly for all years, we are able to create a new item, "miscellaneous," in order to close the gap in our coverage.

Table G–4

VALUE-ADDED OF MINING

(in million 1934 yuan)

	1924	1926	1929	1934	193b	1939	1941
Coal	16.37	18.81	24.12	27.83	32.6	44.71	56.00
Iron ore	5.82	7.90	6.97	8.01	12.6?	21.74	26.17
Gold	3.12	3.26	1.02	0.90	7.5 3	6.82	7.60
Limestone	0.59	0.62	1.44	1.45	1.39	1.53	1.96
Shale oil	—	—	—	0.8	1.64	3.28	5.47
Magnesite	0.11	0.22	0.35	1.11	2.12	6.58	6.68
Salt	6.28	8.52	5.81	4.60	8.63	13.20	13.52
Miscellaneous	1.34	1.63	1.64	1.86	2.78	4.07	4.94
TOTAL	**33.63**	**40.97**	**41.35**	**46.59**	**69.64**	**101.93**	**122.34**

Sources: Computed from the gross values (table G-3) and the ratios of deductible costs (table G-2). The ratio of deductible costs for the item "miscellaneous" is estimated to be roughly 20% on the basis of the information given in [57], 2:52.

H. INDUSTRY

Major Sources of Data

Industrial Surveys. The first extensive industrial survey of all Manchuria was conducted in 1934.[1] A comparable survey covering only the KTLT was made in 1933. The surveys were the joint product of three administrative units: the Kwantung administration, the Manchukuo government, and the South Manchuria Railway Company. The 1934 survey, as well as those conducted in 1936, 1938, 1939, and 1940, covers both the KTLT and the rest of Manchuria and includes all factories employing five or more people.

The surveys contain such detailed industrial statistics as gross value of output, value of raw materials consumed, quantity and value of fuel consumption, wages paid, number of workers, number of man-hours worked, amount of capital paid in, number of machines, and number of establishments. All of the above information is given for each industry and its branches. Gross value-added for each industry can easily be calculated on the basis of the data reported in the surveys.

The type of data reported and the classification of industries remained largely unchanged during the period surveyed. The number of commodity series, however, increased from seventy-six in 1934 to ninety-three in 1936, and to ninety-seven in 1939. In 1934, for example, the seventy-six items were divided into eleven categories as follows (the number of items included in each category is shown in brackets; not all items have been identified here):

(1) Textile products [12]: cotton yarn, cotton cloth, woolen cloth, silk piece goods, dyed cloth.
(2) Metals and related products [7]: metallurgical products, pig iron products, bridge and other construction materials.
(3) Machinery and transport equipment [6]: ordinary machinery, precision equipment, vehicles, ship building.
(4) Building materials [9]: pottery, glass and glass products, ordinary and special bricks, cement, lime.
(5) Chemicals and related products [17]: bean oil and cake, other oils, mineral oil, paints, dyes, pharmaceutical products, paper, ammonia, sulphate, leather, coke.

---

[1] See [69].

71

(6) Foods and beverages [15]: wine and liquor, bean sauce, soft drinks, flour milling, pastry, fishery products, grain husking.
(7) Electrical power [1].
(8) Gas [1].
(9) Wood products [2].
(10) Printing and binding [1].
(11) Miscellaneous [5]: leather products, clothing, matches, cigarettes.

It should be noted that the above classifications have some peculiar features. An outstanding one is the inclusion of the processing of bean oil and cake as a major component of the category "chemicals" (the 1934 survey did not even mention bean cake in this category, but that it is definitely included was established upon further checking). On the other hand, some of the items that could have been included in "chemicals" are included in "miscellaneous." There are essentially no serious omissions of commodities from the seventy-six items reported in the 1934 survey, except for such sundry items as gunny sacks and the like.

These surveys are by far the most extensive industrial data compilation for Manchuria. The joint authorship of three administrative units is indicative of the thoroughness and broad scale of this operation. At the same time, the surveys may contain problems as a result of this joint authorship. On the whole, data reported in the 1934 survey correspond reasonably well to the same type of data reported in the official Kwantung statistics. There are cases, however, in which the two sources disagree significantly. The electrical power industry is a case in point: the figures reported in the 1934 survey are much lower than those indicated in the Kwantung statistics. This is due, in part, to differences in coverage, which we were able to ascertain fairly easily. Discrepancies in value terms may be the result of differences in the price data used, which we have no way of verifying. In this regard, we might also expect differences in collecting techniques, definitions used, and methods of compilation in general. We have therefore approached this source with caution. Attempts have been made to check cases where irregularities are suspected, and alternative data are substituted wherever necessary.

Kwantung Official Statistics. The administration of the KTLT published annual statistics on industry, mining, agriculture, and other sectors, covering both the Kwantung area and the SMR Zone. For our purposes, the *Kantokyoku tokei sanjunenshi* [Statistics of thirty years of the Kwantung administration] (see [25]), a 1937 summary of the annual data from 1910 to 1935, is the basic source of data used. Supplementary data are found in the annual reports.

Industrial statistics from these reports are substantially more limited in scope than those found in the industrial surveys described above. In the first place, there are data on only fifty commodity series, as compared to seventy-four (excluding electrical power and gas to make them comparable) in the 1934 survey. Moreover, they give only value and/or quantity of output and omit data on input.

Price Data. The basic source is the South Manchurian Railway Company's *Manshu keizai tokei nenpo* [Economic statistical yearbook of Manchuria] (see [68]) for various years. Included in this souce are Dairen wholesale prices for individual commodities and indexes for the following eight categories:

(1) Grains: rice, wheat, soybeans, other beans, kaoliang, millet, and wheat flour.

(2) Foods and seasonings: alcoholic beverages, soy sauce, miso, table salt, sugar, tea, and cigarettes.

(3) Meats: beef, pork, chicken, and eggs.

(4) Clothing: ginned cotton, cotton yarn, cotton cloth, and other cloth.

(5) Building materials: cement, bricks, tile and shingles, pig iron, other iron products, lead products, copper ingots, nails, lumber, and tatami.

(6) Fuels: kerosene, coal, wood, charcoal, and matches.

(7) Miscellaneous: bean oil, paper, glass, bean cake, and caustic soda.

(8) Average or composite.

It should be pointed out that while the compilation of industrial statistics for all Manchuria began in the early 1930s, the compilation of price data started much earlier. Price data for major commodities and indexes for major commodity categories are readily available for Dairen and other major cities. According to one report (on the construction of various price indexes in Manchuria, published by the S.M.R. Company in 1941), there were seventeen organizations in Manchuria collecting price and wage data for different time periods. These included the S.M.R. Company, the Chambers of Commerce of nine different cities, the Kwantung administration, several branches of the Manchukuo government, the Bank of Chosen, and others. Discrepancies are thus to be expected.

Estimation Procedures

On the basis of the industrial surveys and the KTLT data, we are able to make gross value and value-added estimates for the whole industrial sector (excluding electrical power) in Manchuria for the following years: 1924, 1926, 1929, 1934, 1936, 1939, and 1941. However, the estimation procedures vary from year to year, depending on the availability of data. Electricity has been singled out because coverage of that item is incomplete in the industrial surveys. Instead of using data from the industrial surveys, we made independent estimates for electrical power output in Manchuria.

Our core year is 1934. This was the first year for which data became available for all of Manchuria, including the KTLT. For years prior to 1934, we must depend on the KTLT statistics in making estimates that apply to Manchuria as a whole. The estimating procedures are detailed below.

(1) A comparison of the KTLT statistics as reported in the 1934 industrial survey and the KTLT official statistics for 1924, 1926, and 1929 reveals that the former have (a) greater product coverage and (b) higher output values for each industry (as well as in the aggregate). For example, the output value of the textile industry in 1934 as reported in the KTLT official statistics is 78.8% of the value recorded in the 1934 survey. An adjustment factor of 1/0.788 is therefore applied to the value of textile industry output for 1924, 1926, and 1929 to derive a value series for the KTLT comparable in coverage to the 1934 industrial survey. Similar adjustment is made for the other industrial branches, with the exception of machinery and transport equipment.[2] The adjusted series are labeled "Adjusted KTLT Gross Values" in table H-1.

(2) The "Adjusted KTLT Gross Values" series are then used as the basis for estimating the "Gross Values in Whole Manchuria" series for the 1920s. This is accomplished by using the 1934 KTLT to Manchuria ratios to expand the KTLT gross values in 1924, 1926, and 1929. In other words, the estimates for the 1920s are made on the assumption that the KTLT/Manchuria ratio for each industry remained unchanged during the period concerned. This procedure may have introduced a serious margin of error if the rates of growth in the two areas were substantially different during this period.

Value-added ratios are computed on the basis of the cost information supplied by the 1934 industrial survey for the whole of Manchuria. It should be noted, however, that there were only two categories of deductible costs (materials and fuels) in the 1934 survey. We have added a third category of miscellaneous deductible costs. The source of this information is the Liu-Yeh study, which in turn depends, in part, on Ou Pao-san's 1933 national income study.

The value-added ratios are then applied to the "Gross Values in Whole Manchuria" series to obtain the value-added figures for 1924, 1926, 1929, and 1934. The results are presented in table H-4.

(3) For the years 1936 and 1939, the gross values and deductible costs for various industrial branches are given in the reports of the industrial surveys made in those years. The estimates of value-added in those two years are presented in table H-5.

(4) We use price deflators to convert all value-added figures in current prices into amounts in 1934 constant prices. The deflator figures are based on

---

[2] For this category, the 1934 annual data for the KTLT constitute only 0.3% of the output value given in the 1934 industrial survey. We therefore use the "metals and related products" rate of growth for 1924-34 as a basis for projecting back to 1924.

the Dairen wholesale price index categories listed above. The kinds of price indexes selected for various industrial branches are as follows:

Industrial Branch	Price Index Used
Textiles	Clothing
Metals	Building materials
Machinery	Building materials
Building materials	Building materials
Chemicals	Miscellaneous
Foods and beverages	Grains
Gas	Fuels
Wood products	Building materials
Miscellaneous	Cigarettes

(5) All value-added figures derived in step (4) are then converted into 1934 constant yuan. There is no industrial survey report for 1941 comparable to the ones we used for earlier years. However, we have collected data on quantities of individual commodities produced in 1939 and 1941 (from [67], no. 3 [1943]) which enable us to construct production indexes for those commodities. The indexes are then used as proxies to derive the value-added of various industrial branches in 1941. Since the indexes refer to physical outputs, no deflation procedure is necessary. The relevant information is presented below:

Industrial Branch	Proxy Used	Output Indexes, 1941/1939
Textiles	Textiles	1.47
Metals	Unweighted average of pig iron and steel	1.06
Machinery	Same	1.06
Building materials	Unweighted average of bricks and cement	0.85
Chemical	Unweighted average of bean oil and cakes	0.72
Foods and beverages	Food	0.81
Gas	Gas	1.31
Wood products	Lumber	1.23

(6) Still remaining is the task of estimating the value-added of the electrical power industry. The industrial survey data do not include the output of government-owned electrical power companies. Therefore, table H-8 is based on our own estimate of value-added in the power industry, adjusted for coverage of all power plants. No deflation procedure is needed in this case because our estimation begins with outputs in physical terms, which are then converted into values by using the 1934 prices.

(7) Value-added figures for the electrical power industry are then added to the estimates obtained in table H-5. The final results are presented in table H-9.

Table H-1

INDUSTRIAL PRODUCTION AND ADJUSTED GROSS VALUES
IN THE KTLT*

(values in thousand current yuan)

Commodities	1924 (1)	1926 (2)	1929 (3)	Official (4)	1934 Industrial Survey (5)	% (6)
Machinery and transport equipment (1)	37	61	123	103	37,845	0.3
	16,198	*20,966*	*32,925*			
Metals and related products (4)	5,055	6,524	10,285	11,815	25,606	46.1
	10,965	*14,152*	*22,310*			
Building materials (4)	5,416	5,790	6,140	6,855	15,347	44.7
	12,116	*12,953*	*13,736*			
Textiles (7)	3,587	12,018	16,102	22,024	27,948	78.8
	4,552	*15,251*	*20,434*			
Chemicals (15)	106,834	129,711	70,835	75,102	93,550	80.3
	133,044	*161,533*	*88,213*			
Food and beverages (11)	56,455	55,045	54,845	31,026	43,338	71.6
	78,848	*76,878*	*76,599*			
Gas (1)	774	1,085	1,176	2,402	3,169	75.8
	1,021	*1,431*	*1,551*			
Wood products (3)	4,855	5,106	5,032	12,283	14,405	85.3
	5,692	*5,986*	*5,899*			
Miscellaneous (3)	3,612	3,471	5,323	7,936	20,180	39.3
	9,191	*8,832*	*13,544*			
TOTAL	186,625	218,811	169,861	169,546	281,388	
	271,627	*317,982*	*275,211*			

* Excluding electricity.

Sources: Cols. (1)–(4): Production values: [25]. Cols. (1)–(3): *Adjusted values:* production values divided by col. (6). For the category "machines and transportation equipment," however, the original figures for 1924–29 are discarded, and the new figures are obtained by extrapolation on the basis of "metals and related products." Col. (5): [69], 1934. Col. (6): Col. (4) divided by col. (5).

Table H-2

GROSS VALUE OF INDUSTRIAL PRODUCTION
IN KTLT AND IN WHOLE MANCHURIA*

(1934 = 100)

	1924	1926	1929	1934	1934 K/M%
Machinery and	*16,198*	*20,966*	*32,925*	*37,845+*	
transport equipment	19,079	24,695	38,781	44,572	84.9%
Metals and	*10,965*	*14,152*	*22,310*	*25,606*	
related products	17,488	22,571	35,582	40,867	62.7%
Building materials	*12,116*	*12,953*	*13,736*	*15,347*	
	16,507	17,647	18,714	20,907	73.4%
Textiles	*4,552*	*15,251*	*20,434*	*27,948*	
	10,586	35,467	47,521	65,020	43.0%
Chemicals	*133,044*	*161,533*	*88,213*	*93,550*	
	175,288	212,823	116,223	123,259	75.9%
Food and beverages	*78,848*	*76,878*	*76,599*	*43,338*	
	148,210	144,507	143,983	81,475	53.2%
Gas	*1,021*	*1,431*	*1,551*	*3,169*	
	1,021	1,431	1,551	3,169	100.0%
Wood products	*5,692*	*5,986*	*5,899*	*14,405*	
	8,006	8,419	8,297	20,267	71.1%
Miscellaneous	*9,191*	*8,832*	*13,544*	*20,180*	
	18,128	17,420	26,714	39,760	50.7%
TOTAL	*271,627*	*317,982*	*275,211*	*281,388*	
	414,313	**484,980**	**437,366**	**439,296**	

* Excluding electricity.

+ Adjusted gross values as derived in table H-1.

Sources: Adjusted gross values in KTLT for 1924-34 are from table H-1. Gross values in whole Manchuria: 1924-29: derived from the KTLT figure, multiplied by the 1934 KTLT percentage of whole Manchuria production; 1934: [69], 1934; 1934 K/M%: the 1934 KTLT production figure divided by the 1934 whole Manchuria production figure.

Table H-3

DEDUCTIBLE COSTS AND VALUE-ADDED OF INDUSTRY

(in percent)

	Materials				Fuels		Miscellaneous deductible costs	Ratio of value-added		
	1934	1936	1939	1934	1936	1939	1934-39	1934	1936	1939
Machinery and transport equipment	55.0	62.5	56.0	2.1	2.6	3.1	2	40.9	32.9	38.9
Metals and related products	73.8	66.1	48.2	1.5	11.4	3.0	2	22.7	20.5	46.8
Building materials	25.3	28.6	30.3	16.8	16.6	16.8	5	52.9	49.8	47.9
Textiles	77.2	81.0	64.6	0.8	1.0	1.0	2	20.0	16.0	32.4
Chemicals	84.9	82.7	81.4	1.3	1.1	2.3	2	11.8	14.2	14.3
Food and beverages	78.0	78.4	66.9	1.6	1.7	2.1	10	10.4	9.9	21.0
Gas	42.2	14.3	15.2	3.9	3.7	4.2	10	43.9	72.0	70.6
Wood products	74.6	75.6	80.8	0.3	0.8	0.8	10	15.1	13.6	8.4
Printing	—	43.8	54.8	—	0.4	0.8	5	—	50.8	39.4
Miscellaneous	60.5	59.9	68.6	0.8	0.5	0.8	5	33.6	34.6	25.6

Sources: Materials and fuels: [69], 1934, 1936, and 1939. Miscellaneous deductible costs: [34], tables F-4 and H-4.

Table H-4

VALUE-ADDED OF INDUSTRY IN WHOLE MANCHURIA*

(in million current yuan)

	1924	1926	1929	1934
Machinery and				
transport equipment	7,803	10,100	15,861	18,230
Metals and				
related products	3,970	5,124	8,077	9,277
Building materials	8,732	9,335	9,900	11,060
Textiles	2,117	7,093	9,504	13,004
Chemicals	20,684	25,113	13,714	14,545
Food and				
beverages	15,414	15,029	14,974	8,473
Gas	448	628	681	1,391
Wood products	1,209	1,271	1,253	3,060
Miscellaneous	6,091	5,853	8,976	13,359
TOTAL	**66,468**	**79,546**	**82,940**	**92,399**

* Excluding electricity.

Sources: Tables H-2 and H-3. The value-added ratio for 1934 is used for all four years.

Table H-5

INDUSTRIAL PRODUCTION IN WHOLE MANCHURIA, 1936 AND 1939*

(in thousand current yuan)

	1936		1939	
	Gross value	Value-added	Gross value	Value-added
Machinery and transport equipment	50,168	16,505	172,386	67,058
Metals and related products	117,362	24,059	401,338	187,826
Building materials	29,183	14,533	98,180	47,028
Textiles	110,647	17,703	287,554	93,167
Chemicals	195,651	27,782	474,999	67,925
Food and beverages	179,754	17,796	413,120	86,755
Gas	4,753	3,422	10,971	7,745
Wood products	26,299	3,577	80,946	6,799
Printing	13,466	6,841	40,084	15,793
Miscellaneous	65,669	22,721	175,073	44,819
TOTAL	**792,952**	**154,939**	**2,154,651**	**624,915**

* Excluding electricity.

Sources: Gross values are from [69], 1936 and 1939. They are converted into value-added figures using the ratios given in table H-3.

Table H–6

PRICE INDEXES OF INDUSTRIAL PRODUCTION

(1934 = 100)

	1924	*1926*	*1929*	*1936*	*1939*
Machinery and					
transport equipment	108.8	98.6	92.4	91.3	213.0
Metals and					
related products	108.8	98.6	92.4	91.3	213.0
Building materials	108.8	98.6	92.4	91.3	213.0
Textiles	162.5	132.4	114.7	97.8	212.2
Chemicals	128.8	117.4	105.5	117.9	193.8
Food and beverages	172.0	146.2	138.5	143.6	245.9
Gas	144.3	131.5	117.5	99.4	162.8
Wood products	108.8	98.6	92.4	91.3	213.0
Miscellaneous	133.2	123.1	115.3	104.3	137.6

Source: [68], various years.

Table H-7

VALUE-ADDED OF INDUSTRY IN WHOLE MANCHURIA*

(in thousand 1934 yuan)

	1924	1926	1929	1934	1936	1939	1941
Machinery and transport equipment	7,172	10,243	17,166	18,230	18,078	31,483	33,371
Metals and related products	3,649	5,197	8,741	9,277	26,352	88,181	93,472
Building materials	8,026	9,467	10,714	11,060	15,918	22,079	18,767
Textiles	1,303	5,357	8,286	13,004	18,101	43,905	64,540
Chemicals	16,059	21,391	12,999	14,545	23,564	35,049	25,235
Food and beverages	8,962	10,280	10,811	8,473	12,393	35,281	28,578
Gas	310	478	580	1,391	3,44?	4,757	6,232
Wood products	1,111	1,289	1,356	3,060	3,913	3,192	3,926
Miscellaneous+	4,573	4,755	7,785	13,359	28,3.	44,049	38,156
TOTAL	**51,165**	**68,457**	**78,438**	**92,399**	**150,1.**	**307,976**	**312,277**

* Excluding electricity.

+ "Miscellaneous" includes printing.

Sources: 1924-39: Derived from tables H-4, H-5, and H-6. 1941: See text.

Table H-8

VALUE-ADDED OF THE ELECTRICAL POWER INDUSTRY IN WHOLE MANCHURIA*

(in million 1934 yuan)

	1924	1926	1929	1934	1936	1939	1941
Quantity							
(in million KWH)	214	295	458	772	1,351	2,534	3,520
Gross value	6.9	9.5	14.8	24.9	43.6	81.8	113.7
Value–added							
ratio (in percent)	41.8	41.8	41.8	41.8	41.8	40.2	40.2
Value–added	**2.88**	**3.97**	**6.19**	**10.41**	**18.22**	**32.88**	**45.71**

* Estimates.

Sources: Quantities: [50], 2:537, and [92], p. 41. Gross values: Quantities multiplied by the 1934 price of 0.0323 yuan per KWH, which is given in [69], 1934. Value–added ratios: The 1936 ratio is used for 1924-36, and the 1939 ratio is used for 1939 and 1941. The two ratios are found in [69], 1936, and [71], 1939. Value–added: Computed from the data above.

Table H-9

VALUE-ADDED OF INDUSTRY IN WHOLE MANCHURIA

(in million 1934 yuan)

	1924	1926	1929	1934	1936	1939	1941
Industry							
(excluding electricity)	51.16	68.46	78.44	92.40	150.11	307.98	312.28
Electricity	2.88	3.97	6.19	10.41	18.22	32.88	45.71
TOTAL	**54.04**	**72.43**	**84.63**	**102.81**	**168.33**	**340.86**	**357.99**

Sources: Figures in the last column of table H-8 are added to the totals in table H-7 to derive value–added totals for all industry in whole Manchuria.

I. SMALL INDUSTRIAL WORKSHOPS

The industrial surveys which we used in section H to estimate industrial output covered only factories employing five or more people. Individual handicraftsmen and workshops with fewer than five employees were numerous, and their contribution to national income was significant. Our estimates of value-added for small industrial workshops begin with the industrial employment data presented in table B-2. The data include the following components: (1) workers in factories employing five or more people; (2) construction workers; and (3) workers in small industrial workshops. If we subtract the first two components from total industrial employment, the remainder represents the last component.

From official sources ([24], 1935, pp. 151-54), we have obtained 1934 daily earnings (in yuan) for eight categories of handicraft workers in three cities:

	Hsinching	Dairen	Fengtien
Carpenter	1.35	1.28	1.38
Mason	1.70	1.17	1.44
Printer	1.25	1.93	1.17
Tailor	1.59	1.77	1.24
Shoemaker	1.60	1.34	1.33
Blacksmith	1.11	1.12	1.19
Bindry worker	1.00	0.90	1.01
Carver	1.28	1.23	1.40

The unweighted average for the twenty-four earning rates above is 1.32 yuan. The average annual earning, based on 250 working days per year at 1.32 yuan per day, is 330 yuan.

We multiply the employment figures derived for workers in small workshops by 330 yuan to obtain annual value-added figures. It should be noted, however, that these earning rates included depreciation charges and factor returns other than wages.

Table I

ESTIMATES OF VALUE-ADDED FOR SMALL WORKSHOPS

(in thousand yuan)

		1934	1936	1939	1941
Industrial workers	(1)	1,041	1,079	1,223	1,425
Factory workers	(2)	189	228	469	505
Construction workers	(3)	130	151	198	245
Workers in small workshops	(4)	722	700	556	675
Value-added of workers in small workshops (in million 1934 yuan)	(5)	238.3	231.0	183.5	222.8

Sources: Row (1): Table B-2. Row (2): 1934 and 1936: [69], 1934 and 1936; 1939: the number of factory workers, excluding those in the electric and gas industries, is given in [70], p. 5, as 439,800. The number of workers in the electric and gas industries in 1941 is given in [37], p. 8, as 40,068. We use this figure and the electricity outputs in 1939 and 1941 (table H-6) to derive 28,849 as the number of workers in the electric and gas industries. The total number of factory workers in 1939 is the sum, i.e., 468,649 (= 439,800 + 28,849). 1941: the number of factory workers, excluding those in the electric and gas industries and those in the KTLT, is given in [69] as 378,510 at the end of 1940. The number of workers in the electric and gas industries was 40,068 in 1941 (see [37], p. 8). The number of factory workers in the KTLT in 1939 is given in [70], p. 11, as 71,208. We know from table B-2 that the total number of industrial workers in the KTLT rose from 91,000 in 1939 to 110,000 in 1941, an increase of 20.9%. We apply the same rate of increase to the factory workers in the KTLT over the two years. The resulting figure is 86,100. The total number of factory workers in 1941 is the sum of these figures: 378,510 + 86,100 + 40,068 = 504,678. Row (3): Col. (1) of table J-1. Row (4): Rows (2) and (3) subtracted from row (1). Row (5): Row (4) multiplied by 330 yuan, which was the average annual earning of workers in small workshops in 1934.

J. CONSTRUCTION

In 1941, the net value-added of the construction sector in Manchuria, excluding the KTLT, is officially recorded as 473.8 million current yuan.[1] Our task here is to (1) add data for the KTLT; (2) add depreciation; and (3) derive estimates for earlier years. Since 88.9% of this 473.8 million yuan was made up of salaries and wages,[2] it is justifiable to use employment data as our basis for estimating value-added. However, employment data for this sector are available only for 1934-41; for 1924-29, we must extrapolate on the basis of the material cost of construction during those years.

A special organization—the Labor Control Committee—was established under the Manchukuo government in December 1933.[3] It recruited construction workers in North China, issued certificates to them, and allowed them to go to Manchuria to work during the construction season. The statistics on construction workers recruited by this committee were separate from those for construction workers supplied locally.[4] The number of construction workers in Manchuria as a whole and the indexes derived from these data for various years are given in table J-1.

For 1924-29, the figures for the material costs of construction are used as a substitute indicator, and the indexes derived from these data are given in table J-2. The two series of indexes are then linked together.

The next question is how to estimate net value-added of construction in the KTLT in 1941, which must then be added to the official figure of 473.8 million yuan mentioned above. According to one source, out of the total 395 million yuan value of construction work done by builders in 1939, about 13.4 million yuan, or 3.4% of the total, can be accredited to the KTLT area.[5] We therefore assume that the net value-added of construction in the KTLT in 1941 was also 3.4% of the total for the whole of Manchuria. Thus, the 473.8 million yuan is increased by this percentage to derive a total of 489.9 million yuan for Manchuria as a whole.

---

[1] See [3], p. 23.
[2] See [3], supp., p. 6.
[3] [1], p. 191, and [40], 1939, p. 360.
[4] [2], p. 30.
[5] [2], 1941, p. 1.

For the construction sector in China in the 1930s, depreciation charges are estimated to be approximately 10% of net value-added.[6] We use the same rate for Manchuria. Thus, the gross value-added of this sector in 1941 would be 538.9 million yuan at current prices. This figure is then applied to the indexes in order to derive value-added figures for other years. All of these figures are then converted into 1934 yuan using the regional annual average wholesale price index of construction materials (214.8%) between 1934 and 1941.[7] The results are presented in table J-3.

It should be pointed out that our estimates include work done by both modern and traditional builders.

---

[0] See [34], p. 588.
[7] [9], 1941, p. 3.

Table J-1

CONSTRUCTION WORKERS IN MANCHURIA, 1934-41

		1934	1936	1939	1941
Local labor	(1)	130,000	150,636	197,515	244,894
Labor recruited by the committee	(2)	162,937	81,849	289,640	273,804
Index	(3)	100.0	79.4	166.3	177.1
TOTAL	**(4)**	**292,937**	**232,485**	**487,155**	**518,592**

Sources: Row (1): 1934: [40], 1933, p. 204; 1936: row (3) - row (2); 1939: [37], 1939, p. 9; 1941: [37], 1941, p. 8. Row (2): 1934: row (3) - row (1); 1936 and 1939: [21], p. 30; 1941: row (3) - row (1). Row (3): 1934 and 1936: [21], p. 186; 1939: row (1) + row (2). This is confirmed by a rough figure of 500,000 estimated by another official source (see [46], 1939, p. 360); 1941: according to [31], p. 23, total wages and salaries paid out by construction firms in 1941 amounted to 237 million yuan, whereas the corresponding figure for individual builders in that year was 192 million yuan. The total employment of construction firms at the end of June 1941 was 286,515 ([45], p. 5). Using this employment figure and the earning figures noted above, we derive 232,077 (= 192/237 x 286,515) for the number of construction workers not affiliated with any construction firm. The total number of construction workers is then 518,592.

Table J-2

MATERIAL COSTS OF CONSTRUCTION

	1924	1926	1929	1934
Amount (in million 1934 yuan)	83.6	88.1	108.1	134.1
Index	62.3	65.7	80.6	100.0

Sources: Kang Chao, Capital Formation in Manchuria, 1920-1945, a forthcoming study.

Table J-3

VALUE-ADDED OF THE CONSTRUCTION SECTOR, 1924-41

	1924	1926	1929	1934	1936	1939	1941
Value-added (in million 1941 yuan)	191.8	202.2	248.1	307.8	244.3	511.9	538.9
Value-added (in million 1934 yuan)	89.3	94.1	115.5	143.3	113.7	238.3	250.9
Index	62.3	65.7	80.6	100.0	79.4	166.3	177.0

Sources: Value-added (1941 yuan): The 473.8 million yuan of net value-added in the construction sector, as given in [3], p. 23, is increased by 3.4% to include the KTLT and by another 10% to include depreciation charges. The resulting amount is then applied to the index numbers. Value-added (1934 yuan): Values in 1941 yuan are deflated by the regional annual average wholesale price index of construction materials between 1934 and 1941, which was 214.8%. Index: Derived by linking the indexes in tables J-1 and J-2.

K. MODERN TRANSPORT AND COMMUNICATIONS

Modern transport is divided into four subsectors: railways, water transport, highway transport, and communications services. For each subsector, output index series (conceptually similar to commodity output series in industry or agriculture) are constructed for selected benchmark years. The methods for constructing such indexes vary, however, depending on the availability and nature of data in each case. Details of the estimating procedures will be explained in the following sections. The four index series for subsectors are then combined to form a series for the modern transport sector as a whole. Finally, this series and the 1941 official estimate of value-added of modern transport are used to derive the value-added of this sector for the other six benchmark years.

Railways

The railway statistics for Manchuria are relatively complete and reliable. We have compiled two time series that represent physical output of railways in Manchuria over this period.

For the period 1929-41, there are data on passenger services (in passenger-kilometers) and freight (in ton-kilometers) for all railways in Manchuria. Data on passenger-kilometers and ton-kilometers in 1924 and 1926 are available only for the South Manchurian Railway. What is available for all railways for these two years is the total number of passengers carried and the total tonnage of freight moved. To convert the number of passengers into passenger-kilometers and the tonnage figures into ton-kilometers, we use the average haul per passenger in 1929 (90 km) and the average haul per ton of freight in the same year (248 km). In essence, this assumes constant average hauls for passengers and freight in those few years. Judging from the data available for 1929-33, this is not an unreasonable assumption. The average hauls were indeed quite stable in 1929-33: from 88 to 104 kilometers for passengers and from 248 to 287 kilometers for freight.

Total revenues of railways in Manchuria from passenger services and freight in 1934 are known to have been 39 million yuan and 155 million yuan, respectively. This information enables us to derive what may be called the "unit gross revenues" as of 1934 for the two railway output series. Thus, we can convert the two output series in physical terms into gross revenue series in 1934 yuan. The results are presented in table K-1.

Water Transport

For water transport, we construct separate output index series for South Manchuria and North Manchuria. In South Manchuria, water transport consisted of the services of harbor facilities, coastal and seagoing transport provided by ships owned by residents or firms in Manchuria, and freight carried by ships on the Liao River. However, even in 1936, less than 1% of the total tonnage of ships arriving in Manchurian ports belonged to local residents or firms.[1] Traffic on the Liao River is also not very significant since, for the most part, that river was not navigable by steamboat. For instance, the annual amount of grain shipped via the Liao River to its seaport Yingkou varied from 36,000 to 63,000 tons in 1930-33.[2] Therefore, we use the quantities of harbor services as a representative "output" series for water transport in South Manchuria. Specifically, the tonnage of ships arriving at all Manchurian harbors in each year is taken as the physical indicator.

There is no seaport in North Manchuria, but there are several navigable rivers—the Sungari, the Amur, and the Neun. Beginning in 1933, statistics on inland water transport in North Manchuria were compiled and published by the Association of Shipping Firms in Harbin, an unofficial organization under the supervision of the S.M.R.[3] Although these statistics included only ships over 20 tons in size and registered with the association, their coverage was quite good. For instance, in 1938, the total freight carried by all ships on North Manchurian rivers was 1,368,000 tons, whereas the total freight reported by the Association was 885,000 tons, which represents a coverage of 65%. Hence, we take the annual total freight as reported by the association as the basic series for 1933-41.

For the years before 1933, the only usable indicator is the total tonnage of ships sailing on the rivers in North Manchuria. Consequently, we use these data as a substitute and construct a series to be linked with the freight index for 1933-41. It should be noted that the two output series for South Manchuria and North Manchuria are far from enough to cover the whole subsector of water transport. They are only two representative series, or indexes, intended primarily to indicate the movement of this subsector over time. In addition, total revenues from water transport in 1934 are known to have been 15.7 million yuan for South Manchuria and 6.5 million yuan for North Manchuria. The two revenue figures may be regarded as the "gross values" produced by

[1] See [50], 1:581.

[2] See [65], 1934, p. 401.

[3] In March 1939 all private ships in North Manchuria were purchased by the S.M.R., and the Association of Shipping Firms in Harbin was dissolved. See [50], 1:625.

water transport in the two regions. The gross revenues are assumed to have changed over time at the rates indicated by the two representative output series. All of the relevant data and computational results are given in table-K-2.

Highways

The use of motor vehicles as a means of public transportation in Manchuria was a new development in the 1930s. In May 1933 a public enterprise was organized under the Bureau of National Railways to set up a network of motor vehicle transportation. Before that date there were only a few private motor vehicles performing trucking or passenger services in Manchuria. Even by 1937, private motor vehicles used for commercial transport carried only 59,000 passengers and 62,000 tons of freight.[4] It is not unreasonable, therefore, to take the volume of freight and passenger services performed by public-owned motor vehicles as a representative output series for this subsector. In other words, production in this subsector is assumed to have begun in 1933. As in the case of the railways, the 1934 revenue figures are used to compute the unit gross values for the two output series. The computations are shown in table K-3.

Communications

The output index for this subsector is again a linked index of two separate series. According to our sources, from 1924 to 1932 the total annual revenues of all communications services in Manchuria were reported, but these were not broken down into separate categories. Even this kind of information is not available for later years. In its place, we use the annual amount of ordinary mail collected by post offices in Manchuria. Since the postal service was by far the most important of all types of available communications services, the margin of error incurred by this procedure is not likely to be substantial.

It should be noted that the gross revenues given here are actually in 1932 yuan. No deflator is needed, however, because no changes in the rates of postage, telegraph, etc., were reported between 1932 and 1934. Our computations are shown in table K-4.

Value-Added for the Modern Transport and Communications Sector as a Whole

All of the gross revenue series for the four subsectors are combined in table K-5 to form a series for the modern transport sector as a whole.

---

[4] See [65], 1939, p. 233.

The next step, then, is to estimate value-added for this sector. According to an official source, net value-added in modern transport in 1941 in Manchuria, excluding the KTLT, was 632.3 million yuan at current prices.[5] This figure does not include 18 million yuan of net value-added for the state-owned communications services, which have been classified as a separate category.[6] Thus, two adjustments must be made: (1) the addition of the state-owned communications services; and (2) the addition of net value-added of this sector for the KTLT. The first adjustment is easy to make: the resulting figure is 650.3 (= 632.3 + 18) million yuan in 1941 prices.

To estimate net value-added of modern transport in Manchuria including the KTLT, we have to use the employment data for 1941. Following the computational methods employed in deriving tables B-1 and B-2 and using the basic data given in [37] (1942, p. 6), and [67] (no. 3 [1943], p. 4), the number of people engaged in modern transport and communications in 1941 is computed as follows:[7]

Manchuria, excluding the KTLT	164,000
KTLT	65,000
Whole Manchuria	229,000

The net value-added of modern transport and communications in all Manchuria is then estimated to be 908 million yuan (= 650.3 x 229/164) for 1941 in current prices.

Since there is no special deflator for this sector, we decided to use the Hsinching (Changchun) wholesale price index between 1934 and 1941, which is 267.6%.[8] The net value-added figure of 908 million yuan for 1941 may thus be converted into 339.3 million 1934 yuan.

The following depreciation rates as percentages of gross revenues have been estimated for China in the 1930s:[9] railways, 3.0%; inland water transport, 5.0%; highway transport, 9.0%; communications services, 0.5%. These rates are used in order to derive gross value-added of the modern transport and communications sector. The results are presented in table K-6.

---

[5] See [3], p. 34.

[6] [3], p. 39.

[7] As pointed out in section B, the coverage of "transport and communications" in the official employment data was changed at some point between 1935 and 1939. Fortunately, the new definition is precisely what we need here. By following the same computational methods used in tables B-1 and B-2, we can derive the figures for this sector in 1941.

[8] Computed from [40], 1942, p. 639, and 1943, p. 693.

[9] See [34], p. 593.

Table K-1

RAILWAYS

	1924	1926	1929	1934	1936	1939	1941
Passenger service							
Passenger-kilometers							
(in millions)	1,626	1,741	2,185	2,544	3,226	8,531	11,006
Gross revenue (in							
million 1934 yuan)	24.9	26.7	33.5	39.0	49.5	130.8	168.7
Freight							
Ton-kilometers							
(in thousands)	6,344	7,145	8,642	9,824	11,013	20,462	25,864
Gross revenue (in							
million 1934 yuan)	100.1	112.7	136.4	155.0	173.8	322.9	408.1

Sources: Quantities: 1924-26: [75], pp. 7-31, gives the total number of passengers carried, which is then multiplied by the average haul of 90 km in 1929, as revealed in [65], 1937, 2:466. Similarly, the total tonnages given in [73] are multiplied by the average haul of 248 km. 1929-36: [65], 1937, 2:466; 1939-41: [50], 1:300. Gross revenues: Total revenues from passenger services and freight in 1934 are given in [51], 1940, p. 268. Unit gross revenue can be derived from these total revenue figures.

Table K-2

WATER TRANSPORT

(in million 1934 yuan)

		1924	1926	1929	1933	1934	1936	1939	1941
South Manchuria									
Ships entering harbors									
(in million tons)	(1)	5,829	6,490	8,272	—	9,445	9,114	6,641	5,220
Index (1934 = 100)	(2)	61.7	68.7	87.6	—	100.0	96.5	70.3	55.3
Gross revenue	(3)	9.7	10.8	13.8	—	15.7	15.2	11.0	8.7
North Manchuria									
Total tonnage of ships									
(in thousand tons)	(4)	116	132	60	124	—	—	—	—
Index (1934 = 100)	(5)	93.5	106.5	48.4	100.0	—	—	—	—
Total freight									
(in thousand tons)	(6)	—	—	—	663	820	846	782	516
Index (1934 = 100)	(7)	—	—	—	80.9	100.0	103.2	95.4	62.9
Linked index									
(1934 = 100)	(8)	75.6	86.2	39.2	—	100.0	103.2	95.4	62.9
Gross revenue	(9)	4.9	5.6	2.5	—	6.5	6.7	6.2	4.1

Sources: Row (1): 1924: [68], 1934, pp. 73, 114; 1926: [68], 1935-36, p. 116; 1929: [65], 1937, 2:466; 1934 and 1936: [65], 1938, p. 12; 1939: [40], 1943, p. 682; 1941: [67], no. 3 (1943), p. 57. Row (2): Derived from row (1). Row (3): 1934 revenue is given in [50], 1:299. This revenue figure is applied to the indexes in row (2). Row (4): [50], 1:308, 626. Row (5): Derived from row (4). Row (6): [73], p. 240, and [50], 1:626. Row (7): Derived from row (6). Row (8): Derived from rows (5) and (7). Row (9): 1934 revenue is given in [50], 1:626. This revenue figure is applied to the indexes in row (8).

Table K-3
HIGHWAY TRANSPORT

	1934	1936	1939	1941
Passenger service				
Passenger-kilometers (in thousands)	19,196	32,985	233,710	284,070
Gross revenue (in million 1934 yuan)	0.85	1.46	10.34	12.58
Freight				
Ton-kilometers (in thousands)	616	875	3,194	4,817
Gross revenue (in million 1934 yuan)	0.36	0.51	1.87	2.81

Sources: Quantities: 1934-39: [50], 1:308; 1941: the number of passengers carried and the number of tons of freight are given in [51], 1944, p. 200. We use the average hauls in 1940, namely, 14.5 km per passenger and 56.4 km per ton of freight, to compute passenger-kilometers and ton-kilometers for 1941. Gross revenues: The revenues from passenger services and freight in 1934 are given in [50], 1:308. Unit gross revenues are derived from those figures, then applied to the passenger- and ton-kilometer totals to derive the gross revenue amounts.

Table K–4

COMMUNICATIONS SERVICES

		1924	1926	1929	1932	1934	1936	1939	1941
Revenue from all communications services (in thousand yuan)	(1)	5,119	5,688	5,986	8,698	—	—	—	—
Index (1932 = 100)	(2)	58.8	65.4	68.8	100.0	—	—	—	—
Collection of ordinary mail (in million pieces)	(3)	—	—	—	111	153	193	283	316
Index (1934 = 100)	(4)	—	—	—	72.5	100.0	126.1	185.0	206.5
Linked index (1934 = 100)	(5)	42.6	47.4	49.9	72.5	100.0	126.1	185.0	206.5
Gross revenue (in million 1934 yuan)	(6)	5.1	5.7	6.0	8.7	12.0	15.1	22.2	24.8

Sources: Row (1): [73], p. 276. Row (2): Derived from row (1). Row (3): 1932: [65], 1934, p. 412; 1934: [68], 1935, p. 177; 1936: [68], 1937, p. 140; 1939 and 1941: [51], 1944, p. 208. Row (4): Derived from row (3). Row (5): Derived from rows (2) and (4). Row (6): Row (5) indexes are applied to the 1932 revenue figures in row (1).

Table K-5

GROSS REVENUE OF MODERN TRANSPORT
AND COMMUNICATIONS
(in million 1934 yuan)

	1924	*1926*	*1929*	*1934*	*1936*	*1939*	*1941*
Railways							
Passenger services	24.9	26.7	33.5	39.0	49.5	130.8	168.7
Freight	100.1	112.7	136.4	155.0	173.8	322.9	408.1
Water transport							
South Manchuria	9.7	10.8	13.8	15.7	15.2	11.0	8.7
North Manchuria	4.9	5.6	2.5	6.5	6.7	6.2	4.1
Highway transport							
Passenger services	—	—	—	0.9	1.5	10.3	12.6
Freight	—	—	—	0.4	0.5	1.9	2.8
Communications	5.1	5.7	6.0	12.0	15.1	22.2	24.8
Index	63.1	70.4	83.7	100.0	114.3	220.2	274.4
TOTAL **Gross Revenue**	**144.7**	**161.5**	**192.2**	**229.5**	**262.3**	**505.3**	**629.8**

Sources: Tables K-1, K-2, K-3, and K-4.

Table K-6

VALUE-ADDED OF MODERN TRANSPORT AND COMMUNICATIONS

(in million 1934 yuan)

	1924	1926	1929	1934	1936	1939	1941
Net value–added	78.0	87.0	103.6	123.7	141.4	272.4	339.3
Depreciation	4.5	5.0	5.9	7.1	8.1	15.7	19.4
TOTAL Gross Value–added	**82.5**	**92.0**	**109.5**	**130.8**	**149.5**	**288.1**	**358.7**

Sources: Net value–added: Obtained by applying 339.3 million yuan for 1941 (see text for this section) to indexes given in table K-5. Depreciation: Obtained by applying the depreciation rates of 3%, 5%, 9%, and 0.5%, respectively, to the total revenues of railways, inland water transport, highway transport, and communications as given in table K-5. Gross value–added: Sum of net value–added and depreciation.

L. TRADITIONAL TRANSPORT

Estimates of value-added are made for the following means of traditional transport in Manchuria in 1924-41.

(1) Porters in the seaports. Porters in the main harbors in Manchuria were controlled by the KTLT authorities. Official records of the work done by porters in terms of man-days are available for some years. For the years for which such data are missing, estimates are made on the basis of total tonnage of imports and exports. The results are shown in tables L-1 and L-2.

(2) Porters serving railways, inland water, and highway transport. To estimate the work done by porters in this subsector, we use the freight data for these means of transport and the tons per man-day figure derived in table L-2. The results are given in table L-3.

In table L-4, the figures for man-days derived in tables L-2 and L-3 for each year are added up and then converted into income using the national average earning of 0.58 yuan per day for porters in Manchuria in 1934.

(3) Rickshaws and horse-drawn passenger carriages. These constituted the primary means of transportation in cities. One official source ([25], p. 577) lists the following numbers of rickshaws and passenger carriages in the KTLT and the SMR Zone:

Year	Rickshaws	Passenger Carriages
1924	3,741	1,507
1926	3,705	1,551
1929	3,709	1,889
1934	4,216	3,078

These vehicles were apparently not displaced by motor vehicles. It is therefore reasonable to assume that in other cities where even fewer motor vehicles were in use, these traditional means of transportation increased in number as urban populations grew. The above data and the population counts in the KTLT and SMR Zone for the period 1924-34 imply that, on the average, there was one rickshaw per 310 city dwellers and one passenger carriage per 593 city dwellers. We use these two ratios and the estimates of urban population in Manchuria as a whole to derive the numbers of rickshaws and passenger carriages.

The daily earning rates of rickshaws and passenger carriages in Dairen in 1934 are given in [84] (1935, p. 140). We assume that there were 200 working days per year for these workers and that the deductible costs, including feed for horses, amounted to 10% of gross revenues for rickshaws and 30% for carriages. We may then derive the following (in 1934 yuan):

	Rickshaws	Passenger Carriages
Daily gross earnings	1.58	2.84
Annual gross earnings	316.00	568.00
Annual net earnings	284.00	398.00

The net figures are then used to compute the value-added of these two types of traditional transport. The results are presented in table L-5.

(4) Horse-drawn freight carts. In Manchuria, horses were used by farmers both for plowing and as a means of transportation. Most farm households owned horse carts. However, their services as owner transportation have already been included in the agricultural production of farmers (see section C). Here we need compute only the value-added of horse carts which were engaged in commercial transport. According to [48] (p. 263), there were 7,000 people professionally engaged in such work in 1941, using a total of 3,400 horse carts. They moved roughly 5.7 million tons of goods per year. Judging from this tonnage figure, these carts must have been in operation year-round. For the years before 1941, we assume that the number of horse carts is linked to total population.

Daily charges in Dairen in 1934 were quoted as 3 yuan for one-horse carts and 4.20 yuan for two-horse carts ([84], 1935, p. 140). The average of 3.60 yuan is taken as the daily gross earning. We further assume that there were 300 working days for each cart in a year and that 30% of the gross earnings was used to cover the costs of operation. Thus, the net annual earning would be 756 yuan. The estimated net earnings for this category in various years are shown in table L-6.

The value-added amounts for the various categories of traditional transport are presented in table L-7.

Table L-1

EXPORTS AND IMPORTS HANDLED BY FOUR SEAPORTS

(in thousand tons)

	1932	1934	1936	1939	1941
Dairen					
Exports	7,203	7,660	5,761	4,802	2,982
Imports	1,465	3,074	3,218	5,338	3,657
Yingkou					
Exports	1,136	1,324	1,188	452	255
Imports	98	354	278	471	290
Lushan					
Exports	240	251	232	91	94
Imports	10	20	12	133	114
Antung					
Exports	29	24	110	41	22
Imports	50	199	60	224	73
TOTAL	**10,231**	**12,906**	**10,859**	**11,552**	**7,487**

Sources: Dairen: [50], 1:602. Yingkou: [50], 1:606. Lushan: 1932: extrapolated using the rates of increase calculated for Yingkou; 1934–41: [50], 1:587, 603, and [66], p. 533. Antung: 1932: extrapolated using the rates of increase calculated for Yingkou; 1934–41: [50], 1:604, and [66], p. 529.

Table L–2

PORTERS IN FOUR SEAPORTS

(in thousand man-days)

	1924	1926	1929	1932	1934	1936	1939	1941
Dairen	2,787	2,800	3,070	2,323	—	—	—	—
Yingkou	140	176	283	509	—	—	—	—
Lushan	115	145	233	111	—	—	—	—
Antung	56	63	60	80	—	—	—	—
TOTAL	**3,098**	**3,184**	**3,646**	**3,023**	**3,796**	**3,194**	**3,398**	**2,202**

Sources: 1924-32: [73], pp. 254, 255. There were no records available for Lushan in 1924 and 1926. To close these data gaps, we use the rates of change in Yingkou for 1924 and 1926 as the basis for extrapolation. 1934-41: According to the data in this table and table L-1 for 1932, we derive a figure of 3.4 tons per man-day. This does not mean that each porter actually carried 3.4 tons of goods per day. It simply shows the average relation between the volume of imports/exports and the work of porters. We use this ratio and the total tonnages in table L-1 to extrapolate totals for 1934-41.

Table L-3

PORTERS SERVING RAILWAYS, INLAND WATERWAYS, AND HIGHWAY TRANSPORT

	1924	1926	1929	1934	1936	1939	1941
Porters (in thousand man-days)	10,543	13,582	17,659	21,461	22,130	35,182	43,556
Freight (in thousand tons)							
Railways	17,304	22,382	29,700	35,658	36,768	58,961	73,444
Inland waterways	620	707	321	820	846	782	516
Highway transport	—	—	—	6	7	67	85
TOTAL	**17,924**	**23,089**	**30,021**	**36,484**	**37,621**	**59,810**	**74,045**

Sources: Porters: Since freight involves loading and unloading, we double the total tonnage of freight in each year and divide it by 3.4 tons per man-day. The latter ratio is the same one used in table L-2. Freight: Railways: [50], 1:301, [73], passim, and [68], 1934, p. 71; inland waterways: table K-2; highway transport: [50], 1:308. For the years 1924-29, the linked indexes are used to derive the estimates given above.

Table L-4

INCOME OF PORTERS

	1924	1926	1929	1934	1936	1939	1941
Porters (in thousand man-days)	13,641	16,766	21,305	25,257	25,324	38,580	45,758
Income (in thousand 1934 yuan)	7,912	9,724	12,357	14,649	14,688	22,376	26,540

Sources: The number of man-days for each year is the sum of the totals in tables L-2 and L-3. The national average daily wage for porters in Manchuria in 1934 was 0.58 yuan. See [83], p. 40.

Table L–5

NET EARNINGS OF RICKSHAWS AND PASSENGER CARRIAGES

(net earnings in thousand 1934 yuan)

	1924	1926	1929	1934	1936	1939	1941
Estimated urban population (in thousands)	5,585	6,106	7,152	8,507	9,276	10,845	12,079
Rickshaws							
Number	18,016	19,697	23,071	27,442	29,923	34,984	38,965
Net earnings	5,116	5,594	6,552	7,793	8,498	9,935	11,066
Passenger carriages							
Number	9,418	10,297	12,061	14,346	15,642	18,288	20,369
Net earnings	3,748	4,098	4,800	5,710	6,226	7,279	8,107
TOTAL NET EARNINGS	**8,864**	**9,692**	**11,352**	**13,503**	**14,724**	**17,214**	**19,173**

Sources: Urban population estimates: These are actually estimates of nonagricultural population. According to [55], p. 97, the proportion of population in 1924 in agriculture, forestry, and animal husbandry was 82%. The residual 18% was taken as the urban population in that year. For 1941, the proportion of population in the former three sectors declined to 73.6% (see [37], p. 1). The residual was then 26.4%. Using these two figures and a linear trend line, we can interpolate the percentages of urban population for the interim years. Rickshaws: A ratio of one rickshaw per 310 urban people and annual net earnings per rickshaw of 284 yuan are used (see the text for this section). Passenger carriages: A ratio of one carriage per 593 urban people and annual net earnings per carriage of 398 yuan are used.

Table L–6

NET EARNINGS OF HORSE CARTS

	1924	1926	1929	1934	1936	1939	1941
Population index	67.8	71.0	78.2	84.5	87.4	94.1	100.0
Number of horse carts	2,305	2,414	2,659	2,873	2,972	3,199	3,400
Net earnings (in thousand 1934 yuan)	1,743	1,825	2,010	2,172	2,247	2,418	2,570

Sources: Horse carts: The 1941 figure used here is given in [65], p. 263. This figure is applied to the population indexes to derive the figures for other years. Net earnings: The number of carts multiplied by 756 yuan (see the text for this section).

Table L–7

VALUE-ADDED OF TRADITIONAL TRANSPORT

(in million 1934 yuan)

	1924	1926	1929	1934	1936	1939	1941
Porters	7.9	9.7	12.4	14.7	14.7	22.4	26.5
Rickshaws and passenger carriages	8.9	9.7	11.4	13.5	14.7	17.2	19.2
Horse carts	1.7	1.8	2.0	2.2	2.2	2.4	2.6
TOTAL	**18.5**	**21.2**	**25.8**	**30.4**	**31.6**	**42.0**	**48.3**

Sources: Tables L-4, L-5, and L-6.

M. TRADE

The trade sector is a highly heterogeneous one. In the official compilation of national income for 1941, this sector includes: commodity selling, wholesale and retail; financial and insurance firms; real estate and commodity rentals;[1] entertainment and show business; services such as restaurants, hotels, barbers, etc.; and brokers and agents.[2] The coverage of trade in the employment surveys is the same. Lacking a better alternative, we attempt to estimate the value-added of this sector by the following procedures.

(1) The official estimate of net value-added of trade in 1941, excluding the KTLT, was 1,762.7 million yuan.[3] It is raised here by 5.5% to 1,859.6 million yuan because the employment in trade in the KTLT was 5.5% of that in the rest of Manchuria in that year (see table B-2).

(2) For 1934-41, we use the employment indexes as a substitute for the output series of that sector. The results are shown in table M-1.

(3) For 1924-29, we use the gross revenues of domestic freight transport (not the value of goods shipped, which is not known) as the indicator of changes in trade volume. This series is then linked to the employment index. The results are presented in table M-2.

(4) The net value-added in 1941 is increased by 7.3% to include depreciation charges.[4] The resulting figure is the gross value-added amount for that year.

(5) The amount of gross value-added in 1941 is applied to the indexes in order to obtain value-added estimates for other years. The resulting figures are then deflated by the overall wholesale price index in Hsinching between 1934 and 1941.

---

[1] This category includes only the commissions received by real-estate agents and firms. House rentals as income will be treated separately (see section O).

[2] Brokers and go-betweens were quite common when open markets for many articles had not been developed. They matched sellers to buyers and charged commissions.

[3] See [3], p. 25.

[4] 7.3% was the rate for some Chinese firms in 1933. See [34], p. 604.

Table M-1

NUMBER OF PEOPLE ENGAGED IN TRADE

(in thousands)

	1934	1936	1939	1941
Manchuria (excluding KTLT)	1,144	1,200	1,445	1,514
KTLT	63	79	79	83
Index	100.0	106.0	126.3	132.3
TOTAL	**1,207**	**1,279**	**1,524**	**1,597**

Source: Table B-2.

Table M-2

GROSS REVENUE OF DOMESTIC FREIGHT

(in million 1934 yuan)

	1924	1926	1929	1934
Railways	100.1	112.7	136.4	155.0
Inland waterways	4.9	5.6	2.5	6.5
Traditional transport	1.7	1.8	2.0	2.2
Index	65.2	73.4	86.1	100.0
TOTAL	**106.7**	**120.1**	**140.9**	**163.7**

Sources: Tables K-1, K-2, and L-7. The figures for traditional transport are the value–added figures for horse carts.

Table M–3

VALUE-ADDED OF TRADE

	1924	1926	1929	1934	1936	1939	1941
Million 1941 yuan	983.3	1,107.0	1,298.5	1,508.2	1,598.7	1,904.9	1,995.4
Million 1934 yuan	367.4	413.7	485.2	563.6	597.4	711.8	745.6

Sources: See the text for this section. The deflator used (267.6%) is the overall wholesale price index in Hsinching between 1934 and 1941, as given in [40], 1942, p. 639, and 1943, p. 693.

N. PROFESSIONALS, GOVERNMENT EMPLOYEES, HOUSEHOLD SERVICES, AND OTHER OCCUPATIONS

The value-added of the following three groups of people, according to the official employment classification listed in table B-2, remains to be estimated: (1) professionals and government employees; (2) household services; and (3) other occupations.

The first category contains seven subgroups of professionals plus government employees other than those in the armed forces. The seven subgroups of professionals are: (a) people engaged in religious work; (b) educational workers; (c) medical workers; (d) people engaged in the practice of law; (e) writers, artists, and musicians; (f) clerks; and (g) other professionals. A definition for "clerks" is in order. They were neither secretaries in government and business offices nor clergymen in churches. Rather, they were self-employed and provided handwriting and hand-copying services at piece rates, mainly for the illiterate. The official source ([3], supp., pp. 25-26) contains sample studies for the first five subgroups of professionals listed above, showing their average net earnings in 1941. There is no information about the average earnings of clerks, other professionals, and government employees. We simply group them together and assume that their average earnings in 1941 were about equal to that of people engaged in educational work (518 yuan per year). The six earning rates are then weighted by the number of people engaged in those occupations in 1941 in order to obtain a weighted average earning rate for the whole category. This step is necessary because there are no similar earning data for this heterogeneous category for other years, and so we must apply the 1941 weighted average earning rate to other years. The results are given in table N-1.

Both "household services" and "other occupations" are low-income employment. The latter, as explained in section B, contains mainly members of the armed forces. From the total number of people in the two categories as given in section B and their total earnings in 1941 (as given in [3], p. 38), an average annual earning rate of 185 yuan is derived. However, this average earning rate is believed to be an understatement because both categories received payments in kind in addition to their cash earnings. Practically all servants (household services) were provided with room and board; soldiers had housing, meals, and uniforms. In view of their low cash earnings, these payments in kind were relatively significant. Income in kind, including meals, housing, and clothing (if applicable), is imputed to be 115 yuan for each person employed. This sum is about equal to the value of 500 kilograms of kaoliang during that period; kaoliang was the main grain consumed by low-income people in Manchuria at that time.[1] Thus, the per capita earning is increased from 185 yuan to 300 yuan.

We use the employment data for the three categories and their earning rates in 1941, as explained above, to compute value-added figures for 1934, 1936, 1939, and 1941. These figures are in 1941 yuan and must therefore be converted into 1934 yuan using the cost of living index (273.9%) in Hsinching between 1934 and 1941.[2]

Total depreciation of fixed assets of medical work and law offices is presumably a small amount and is not taken into account here.

---

[1] The price of kaoliang was 11.37 yuan per 50 kg in Hsinching in 1941. See [9], 1941, p. 11.

[2] This is a linked index derived from the Hsinching cost of living indexes given in various issues of [86].

Table N-1

AVERAGE EARNINGS OF PROFESSIONAL EMPLOYEES

(in 1941 yuan)

Occupation		Average earnings	Weight
Religious work	(1)	2,596	7.1
Educational work	(2)	518	8.3
Medical work	(3)	12,978	4.9
Law practice	(4)	3,346	0.9
Writers, artists, and musicians	(5)	3,016	1.8
Government employees and other professionals	(6)	518	77.0
Weighted average	(7)	1,350	

Sources: Average earnings: Rows (1)–(5) are computed from the information given in [3], supp., pp. 25–26. Row (6) is assumed to be the same as row (2). Weights: Percentages computed from the numbers of people in those groups, as given in [37], 1942, p. 8.

Table N-2

VALUE-ADDED FOR EMPLOYEES

(numbers in thousands,

value-added in million 1941 yuan)

	1934	1936	1939	1941
Government employees				
and professionals (#)	416	454	954	1,180
(value–added)	561.6	612.9	1,287.9	1,593.0
Household services (#)	388	399	567	501
(value–added)	116.4	119.7	170.1	150.3
Other occupations (#)	477	479	932	1,042
(value–added)	143.1	143.7	279.6	312.6
TOTAL VALUE–ADDED				
(in million 1941 yuan)	**821.1**	**876.3**	**1,737.6**	**2,055.9**
(in million 1934 yuan)	**299.8**	**319.9**	**634.4**	**750.6**

Sources: The employment data are from table B-2. The average annual earning rate in 1941 was 1,350 yuan for government employees and professionals (see table N-1). It was 300 yuan for both household services and other occupations (see text). The deflator used is 273.9%. For the years 1924-29, total value-added of these groups is assumed to be 10% of the GDP (see section A).

O. IMPUTED RESIDENTIAL RENTS

The standard practice for national income accounting is to include both the cash rent income from residential houses and the imputed rent income of owner-occupied dwellings. This may be estimated either from the data on the stock of residential houses or from sample studies of family budgets.

A thorough sample study of rural household budgets was conducted by the Manchukuo government in 1934.[1] One item reported in the survey was the rental cost for residence, expressed as a percentage of total cost of living. These results are reproduced in table O-1. We believe that the percentages for the eleven localities surveyed must be too low. The survey lumped together all households in a locality and recorded only actual rental payments by those who did not own houses, excluding altogether the imputed rent of owner-occupied houses. According to another survey of the rural economy by the S.M.R. in 1932, households occupying rented houses accounted for 42.8% of the rural households surveyed.[2] A similar survey was done by the Manchukuo government two years later (1936). In this survey, the imputed rent was included.[3] The results, as presented in the 1936 figures of table O-1, yield a weighted average (with numbers of households as weights) of 6.32% of total living expenses. The proportions of actual and imputed rents were as follows:

Location	Actual rent	Imputed rent
Faku	63.8%	36.2%
Tehui	15.8%	84.2%
Itung	77.2%	22.8%

While there are no similar studies on family budgets for the urban population in Manchuria, one can safely assume that rental expenses as a percentage of income must be higher in cities than in rural communities. This would be so because housing is likely to be an income-elastic item before per capita income reaches a high level and because both the quality and construction costs of urban dwellings are higher. Our rough estimate of rental expenses for the urban population in Manchuria during this period is at least 10% greater than

---

[1] See various volumes of [47].
[2] [22], p. 73.
[3] See the definitions and explanations of the surveyed items in [46], p. 5.

our estimate for the rural population. The weighted average for both urban and rural populations would then be 7.1%.[4]

We subtract 15% of the gross rents as operational costs.[5] Therefore, residential rents, actual as well as imputed, would account for about 6.3% (= 7.1% x 85% of gross rents) of total disposable income, or 5.7% of gross domestic product.[6] We apply the latter rate to the GDP in the seven years covered in the study. The resulting estimates are listed in table O-2.

---

[4] The proportion of agricultural population in Manchuria was 82% in 1924 (see [55], p. 97) but declined to 74% in 1941 (see [37], p. 1). There were also nonagricultural people living in rural communities. We take 80% as the weight for the rural population and 20% for the urban population.

[5] This percentage is taken from [34], p. 610.

[6] According to [3], p. 7, taxes were 6.4% of disposable income in 1941 in Manchuria; [34], p. 66 gives total depreciation as 3.5% of NDP in China in 1933. We use these two ratios to derive our formula for rental expenses as a percentage of GDP: (6.3%/106.4%)/103.5% = 5.7%.

Table O–1

RENTAL PAYMENTS OF RURAL HOUSEHOLDS

Hsien	Number of households surveyed	House rental payment as % of total living expenses
1934		
Chingkang, Pinchiang	30	0.70
Lansi, Pinchiang	42	1.10
Anta, Pinchiang	24	1.44
Chaochow, Pinchiang	62	0.84
Fuyu I, Lungchiang	19	1.20
Fuyu II, Lungchiang	13	3.26
Naho, Lungchiang	34	1.10
Paichuan, Lungchiang	33	8.60
Mingsui, Lungchiang	43	1.00
Keshan, Lungchiang	18	2.12
Lungchen, Lungchiang	34	3.70
1936		
Faku, Fengtien	37	5.00
Tiehlen, Fengtien	41	4.00
Tehui, Kirin	33	8.03
Itung, Kirin	24	10.00

Sources: 1934: [47], various *hsien* volumes, pages as follows: Chingkang, p. 79; Lansi, p. 186; Anta, p. 268; Chaochow, p. 394; Fuyu I, p. 50; Fuyu II, p. 100; Naho, p. 162; Paichuan, p. 228; Mingsui, p. 310; Keshan, p. 408; Lungchen, p. 484. 1936: [46], various *hsien* volumes, pages as follows: Faku, p. 170; Tiehlen, p. 327; Tehui, p. 205; and Itung, p. 253.

Table O-2

VALUE-ADDED FOR RESIDENTIAL RENT

(in million 1934 yuan)

Year	Value-added
1924	133.8
1926	150.5
1929	170.3
1934	152.6
1936	187.5
1939	238.0
1941	269.8

Source: See the text for this section.

BIBLIOGRAPHY

The numbers enclosed in brackets to the left of each entry are the source code numbers used throughout sections A-O.

[1]   Architectural Society. *Manshū kenchiku gaisetsu* [Introduction to architecture in Manchuria]. Hsinching, 1940.

[2]   Association of Civil Engineering and Construction Industry in Manchuria. *Tōkei nenpō* [Statistical yearbook]. Dairen, serial.

[3]   Association of Survey Research Organizations in Manchuria. *Manshūkoku kokumin shotoku chōsa sho, 1941* [Survey report of the national income of Manchukuo, 1941]. Hsinching, 1941.

[4]   Bank of Taiwan. *Jih-chu shih-tai Tai-wan ching-chi chih te-cheng* [Features of Taiwan's economy during the period of Japanese occupation]. Taipei, 1957.

[5]   ————. *Jih-chu shih-tai Tai-wan mi-ku-ching-chi lun* [The rice economy of Taiwan during the period of Japanese occupation]. Taipei, 1969.

[6]   ————. *Jih-pen ti-kuo-chu-i hsia chih Tai-wan* [Taiwan under Japanese imperialism]. Taipei, 1956.

[7]   ————. *Tai-wan ching-chi shih* [Economic history of Taiwan]. Taipei, 1959.

[8]   Buck, John L. *Land Utilization in China*. Nanking, 1937.

[9]   Central Bank of Manchuria. *Manshū bukka nenpō* [Price yearbook of Manchuria]. Hsinching, serial.

[10]   ————. *Manshū ni okeru manjin Chūshō shōkōgyō sha gyotai chōsa* [Survey of small and medium Chinese traders and industrial producers in Manchuria]. Hsinching, 1938.

[11]   Chang Cheng-ta. *Tung-pei ching-chi* [The economy of the northeastern region]. Taipei, 1954.

[12]   Chang Chung-ho, and Huang Wei-i. *Tsu-kuo ti hsu-mu yu hsu-chan tzu-yuan* [Husbandry resources and products in China]. Shanghai, 1953.

122

[13] Chen Nai-ruenn. *Chinese Economic Statistics*. Chicago, 1967.

[14] Cheng Hsueh-chia. *Tung-pei ti kung-yeh* [Industry in the northeastern region]. Shanghai, 1946.

[15] Cohen, Jerome B. *Japan's Economy in War and Reconstruction*. Minneapolis, 1949.

[16] Dairen Chamber of Commerce and Industry. *Manshū yunyū honpōhin to takokuhin to no kyōsō jijō* [Competition between imports from Japan and imports from other countries in Manchuria]. Dairen, 1932.

[17] Fushun Coal Mine Company. *Fu-shun tan-kuang ching-fei t'ung-chi* [Budgetary statistics of the Fushun Coal Mine]. Fushun, 1939.

[18] Hashitsume Kanichi. *Manshū sangyō kaihatsu to rōdōsha nōmin jōtai* [Industrial development in Manchuria and agricultural laborers]. Tokyo, 1936.

[19] Hori Tsuneo. *Manshūkoku keizai no kenkyū* [Study of the economy of Manchukuo]. Tokyo, 1942.

[20] Japanese Government. *Shōwa gonen kokusei chōsa saishū hōkokusho* [Final report of the 1930 census]. Tokyo, 1938.

[21] Jones, Francis C. *Manchuria Since 1931*. London, 1949.

[22] Kantō Kyoku. *Kannai Shinajin no nōgyō keizai* [Farm economy of the Chinese in the district]. Dairen, 1932.

[23] ———. *Kantō kyoku jinkō dōtai tōkei* [Population statistics of the Kwantung territory]. Dairen, serial.

[24] ———. *Kantō kyoku bukka chingun chōsa nenpō* [Yearbook of prices and wages]. Dairen, serial.

[25] ———. *Kantō kyoku tōkei sanjunenshi* [Thirty years' statistics for the Kwantung administration]. Dairen, 1937.

[26] ———. *Kantō kyoku tōkei sho* [Statistics of the Kwantung territory]. Dairen, serial.

[27] ———. *Shōwa junen kantō kyoku kokusei chōsa* [Report of the 1935 census for the Kwantung territory]. Dairen, 1939.

[28] Keizai Tōkei Nenkan Sha. *Keizai tōkei nenkan* [Yearbook of economic statistics]. Tokyo, serial.

[29] Kuznets, Simon. *Economic Growth of Nations*. Cambridge, Mass., 1971.

[30] ———. *Modern Economic Growth*. New Haven, 1966.

[31] Lee, Robert H. G. *The Manchurian Frontier in Ching History*. Cambridge, Mass., 1970.

[32] Li Wen-chih et al. *Chung-kuo chin-tai nung-yeh shih tzu-liao* [Historical materials on agriculture in modern China]. Peking, 1957.

[33] Lien Chun. *Tung-san-sheng ching-chi shih-kuang lan-yao* [Economic compendia of Manchuria]. Shanghai, 1931.

[34] Liu, T. C., and K. C. Yeh. *The Economy of the Chinese Mainland, National Income and Economic Development, 1933-59*. Princeton, 1965.

[35] Manchukuo Government. *Manshū kenkoku jūnenshi* [Ten years of Manchukuo]. Reprint, Tokyo, 1969.

[36] ———. *Man-chu-kuo nien-pao* [Yearbook of Manchukuo]. Hsinching, serial.

[37] ———. *Man-chu ti-kuo hsien-chu jen-kou t'ung-chi* [Population statistics of Manchukuo]. Hsinching, serial.

[38] ———. *Manshūkoku fugyō chōsa sho* [Survey report of subsidiary production]. Hsinching, 1937.

[39] ———. *Manshūkoku gaikoku bōeki tōkei nenpō* [Statistical yearbook of the foreign trade of Manchukuo]. Hsinching, serial.

[40] ———. *Manshūkoku gensei* [Present conditions of Manchukuo]. Hsinching, serial.

[41] ———. *Manshūkoku sangyō gaikan* [Compendia of Manchurian industry]. Mukden, 1937.

[42] ———. *Manshūkoku shōgyō jittai chōsa sho* [Survey report of commerce in Manchukuo]. Hsinching, 1942.

[43] ———. *Manshū nōgyō yōran* [Compendia of Manchurian agriculture]. Hsinching, 1940.

[44] ———. *Manshū tikoku kairan* [Compendia of the Manchu Empire]. Hsinching, serial.

[45] ———. *Manshū tikoku tōkei geppō* [Monthly statistical report of the Manchu Empire]. Hsinching, serial.

[46] ———. *Nōgyō jittai chōsa hōkoku sho, 1936* [Survey report of agriculture, 1936]. Hsinching, 1936.

[47] ———. *Nōsan chōsa jittai--1934* [Survey of farm economy—1934]. Hsinching, 1937.

[48] Manchuria Information Bureau. *Manshū jijō--suisan* [Conditions in Manchuria—marine products]. Tokyo, 1935.

[49] Manmō Bunka Kyokai. *Manmō zensho* [Encyclopedia of Manchuria and Mongolia]. Dairen, 1922.

[50] Manshikai. *Manshū kaihatsu yonjūnenshi* [The history of forty years' development in Manchuria]. Tokyo, 1964.

[51] Manshu Daily News. *Manshū nenkan* [Yearbook of Manchuria]. Dairen, serial.

[52] Manshūkoku Tsushinsha. *Manshū keizai jūnenshi* [Ten years of the Manchurian economy]. Tokyo, 1942.

[53] *Manshū tikoku dai kuan* [A general view of the Manchu Empire]. Tokyo, 1937.

[54] Matsuzaki Yujiro. *Ho shi keizai kaihatsu ron--santōsei no zai ninshiki* [A treatise on the economy of North China—Shantung Province]. Tokyo, 1941.

[55] National Northeastern University. *Tung-pei yao-lan* [Compendia of the northeastern region]. Chungking, 1944.

[56] Nippon Gakujutsu Shinkokai. *Manshū no bokuyō* [Sheep husbandry in Manchuria]. Tokyo, 1936.

[57] Ou Pao-san. *Chung-kuo kuo-min so-te, 1933* [China's national income, 1933]. Shanghai, 1947.

[58] Pauley, E. W. *Report on Japanese Assets in Manchuria to the President of the United States.* Washington, 1946.

[59] Sadako Ogata. *Defiance in Manchuria--The Making of Japanese Foreign Policy, 1931-1932.* Berkeley, 1964.

[60] Shen Hsueh-yuan. *Tung-san-sheng wu-chan tzu-yuan yu hua-hsueh kung-yeh* [Resources and the chemical industry in the three eastern provinces]. Shanghai, 1936.

[61] Sino–Japanese Culture Association. *Manmō nenkan* [Yearbook of Manchuria and Mongolia]. Dairen, serial.

[62] Society of Far East Studies. *Manshūkoku sangyō yōran* [Compendia of Manchurian industry]. Tokyo, 1938.

[63] South Manchuria Railway Company. *Contemporary Manchuria*. Dairen, serial.

[64] ———. *Manjin nōka keizai chōsa hōkoku* [Economic survey of Manchurian farm families]. Dairen, 1938.

[65] ———. *Manshū keizai nenpō* [Economic yearbook of Manchuria]. Tokyo, serial.

[66] ———. *Manshū keizai teiyō* [Compendia of the Manchurian economy]. Dairen, 1938.

[67] ———. *Manshū keizai tōkei kihō* [Economic statistical quarterly of Manchuria]. Dairen, serial.

[68] ———. *Manshū keizai tōkei nenpō* [Economic statistical yearbook of Manchuria]. Dairen, serial.

[69] ———. *Manshū kōjō tōkei* [Manchurian factory statistics]. Dairen, serial.

[70] ———. *Manshū kōjō tōkei kaisetsu* [Explanations of Manchurian factory statistics]. Dairen, 1942.

[71] ———. *Manshū kōjō tōkei sokuhō* [Summary of Manchurian factory statistics]. Dairen, 1939.

[72] ———. *Manshūkoku kokumin shotoku narabi ni kokufu keisansho, 1930* [Accounts of national income and national wealth of Manchuria, 1930]. Dairen, 1930.

[73] ———. *Manshū kōtsū tōkei shūsei* [Compilation of transportation statistics of Manchuria]. Dairen, 1935.

[74] ———. *Manshū ni okeru gyogyō narabi ni suisanbutsu jukyū jōkyō chōsa hakokusho* [Survey report on the demand and supply of marine products in Manchuria]. Dairen, 1933.

[75] ———. *Manshū ni okeru kaju narabi ni sosai* [Fruits and vegetables in Manchuria]. Dairen, 1935.

[76] ———. *Manshū ni okeru jidōsha yusō kikan no genjo kyo sono shōrai* [The present and future of the automobile transportation system in Manchuria]. Dairen, 1928.

[77] ———. *Manshū ni okeru koryoshu jōzōgyō* [The brewery industry in Manchuria]. Dairen, 1930.

[78]   ———. *Manshū ni okeru sei fun gyō* [The flour-milling industry in Manchuria]. Dairen, 1924.

[79]   ———. *Manshū ni okeru yubogyō* [The soybean oil industry in Manchuria]. Dairen, 1924.

[80]   ———. *Manshū no kōgyō* [The mining industry in Manchuria]. Dairen, 1933.

[81]   ———. *Manshū no kuri* [Coolies in Manchuria]. Dairen, 1934.

[82]   ———. *Manshū nōsan tōkei* [Agricultural statistics of Manchuria]. Dairen, 1943.

[83]   ———. *Manshū rōdō jijō shuran* [Labor force in Manchuria]. Dairen, 1936.

[84]   ———. *Manshū sangyō tōkei* [Manchurian industrial statistics]. Dairen, serial.

[85]   ———. *Manshū shōkō jijō* [Industry and commerce in Manchuria]. Dairen, serial.

[86]   ———. *Mantetsu chōsa geppō* [Monthly of the S.M.R. surveys]. Dairen, serial.

[87]   ———. *Nōka keizai chōsa* [Economic survey of farm families]. Dairen, 1936.

[88]   ———. *Report on Progress in Manchuria.* Dairen, serial.

[89]   ———. *Shina no jukoku to naman no sanko* [Chinese junks and the three ports in South Manchuria]. Dairen, 1927.

[90]   ———. *Shina no kōjō jijō* [Chinese industrial survey]. Dairen, 1928.

[91]   State Statistical Bureau. *Ten Great Years.* Peking, 1960.

[92]   ———. *Wo-kuo kang-t'ieh tien-li mei-tan chi-hsieh fang-chih tsao-chih kung-yeh ti chin-hsi* [The present and past of our iron and steel, power, coal, machine-building, textile, and paper-manufacturing industries]. Peking, 1958.

[93]   Sun, Kungtu C. *The Economic Development of Manchuria in the First Half of the Twentieth Century.* Cambridge, Mass., 1969.

[94]   Supreme Command for the Allied Powers. *Summation.* Tokyo, serial.

[95]   Takekiko, Yoshihashi. *Conspiracy at Mukden--The Rise of the Japanese Military.* New Haven, 1963.

[96]   Tang, Peter S. H. *Russian and Soviet Policy in Manchuria and Outer Mongolia, 1911-1931.* Durham, 1959.

[97]   *Tung-pei nien-chien, 1931* [Yearbook of the northeastern region, 1931]. Shenyang, 1931.

[98]   Tung-pei Wu-tzu Tiao Chieh Wei-yuan-hui. *Tung-pei ching-chi hsiao-tsung-shu liang-chung* [Two studies of the Manchurian economy]. Taipei, 1971.

[99]   United Nations, Department of Economic and Social Affairs. *Population Studies,* no. 25. New York, 1956.

[100] ———. *Yearbook of National Accounts Statistics.* New York, serial.

[101] Wang Feng-jui.   *Tung-pei chih chiao-t'ung* [Transportation in Manchuria]. Taipei, 1968.

MICHIGAN PAPERS IN CHINESE STUDIES

No. 2. *The Cultural Revolution: 1967 in Review*, four essays by Michel Oksenberg, Carl Riskin, Robert Scalapino, and Ezra Vogel.

No. 3. *Two Studies in Chinese Literature*, by Li Chi and Dale Johnson.

No. 4. *Early Communist China: Two Studies*, by Ronald Suleski and Daniel Bays.

No. 5. *The Chinese Economy, ca. 1870-1911*, by Albert Feuerwerker.

No. 7. *The Treaty Ports and China's Early Modernization: What Went Wrong?* by Rhoads Murphey.

No. 8. *Two Twelfth Century Texts on Chinese Painting*, by Robert J. Maeda.

No. 9. *The Economy of Communist China, 1949-1969*, by Chu-yuan Cheng.

No. 10. *Educated Youth and the Cultural Revolution in China*, by Martin Singer.

No. 11. *Premodern China: A Bibliographical Introduction*, by Chun-shu Chang.

No. 12. *Two Studies on Ming History*, by Charles O. Hucker.

No. 13. *Nineteenth-Century China: Five Imperialist Perspectives*, selected by Dilip Basu and edited by Rhoads Murphey.

No. 14. *Modern China, 1840-1972: An Introduction to Sources and Research Aids*, by Andrew J. Nathan.

No. 15. *Women in China: Studies in Social Change and Feminism*, edited by Marilyn B. Young.

No. 17. *China's Allocation of Fixed Capital Investment, 1952-1957*, by Chu-yuan Cheng.

No. 18. *Health, Conflict, and the Chinese Political System*, by David M. Lampton.

No. 19. *Chinese and Japanese Music-Dramas*, edited by J. I. Crump and William P. Malm.

No. 21. *Rebellion in Nineteenth-Century China*, by Albert Feuerwerker.

No. 22. *Between Two Plenums: China's Intraleadership Conflict, 1959-1962*, by Ellis Joffe.

No. 23. *"Proletarian Hegemony" in the Chinese Revolution and the Canton Commune of 1927*, by S. Bernard Thomas.

No. 24. *Chinese Communist Materials at the Bureau of Investigation Archives, Taiwan*, by Peter Donovan, Carl E. Dorris, and Lawrence R. Sullivan.

No. 25. *Shanghai's Old-Style Banks (Ch'ien-chuang), 1800-1935*, by Andrea Lee McElderry.

No. 26. *The Sian Incident: A Pivotal Point in Modern Chinese History*, by Tien-wei Wu.

MICHIGAN ABSTRACTS OF CHINESE AND JAPANESE WORKS ON CHINESE HISTORY

No. 1. *The Ming Tribute Grain System*, by Hoshi Ayao, translated by Mark Elvin.

No. 2. *Commerce and Society in Sung China*, by Shiba Yoshinobu, translated by Mark Elvin.

No. 3. *Transport in Transition: The Evolution of Traditional Shipping in China*, translated by Andrew Watson.

No. 4. *Japanese Perspectives on China's Early Modernization: A Bibliographical Survey*, by K. H. Kim.

No. 5. *The Silk Industry in Ch'ing China*, by Shih Min-hsiung, translated by E-tu Zen Sun.

No. 6. *The Pawnshop in China*, by T. S. Whelan.

Michigan Papers and Abstracts available from:

Center for Chinese Studies
The University of Michigan
104 Lane Hall (Publications)
Ann Arbor, Michigan 48109 USA